SEEING LANDSCAPES

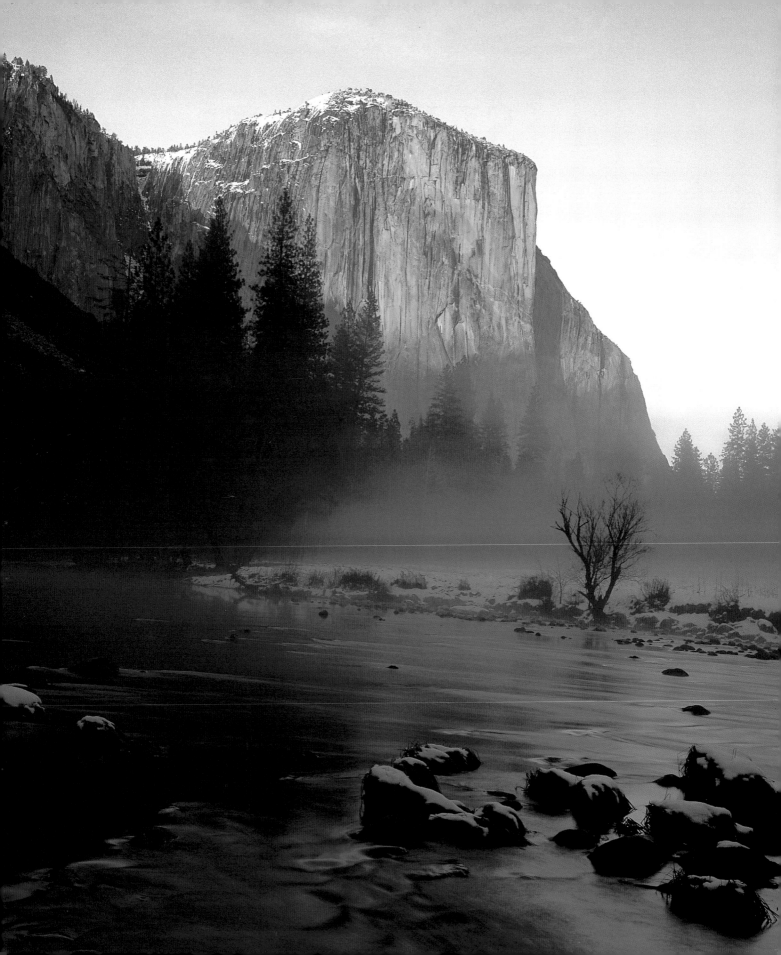

SEEING LANDSCAPES

The Creative Process Behind Great Photographs

CHARLIE WAITE

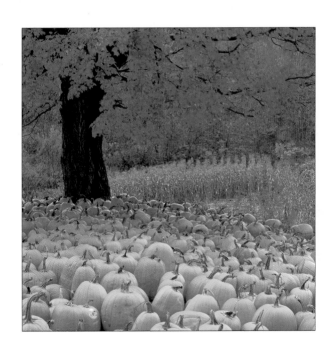

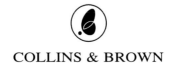

COLLINS & BROWN

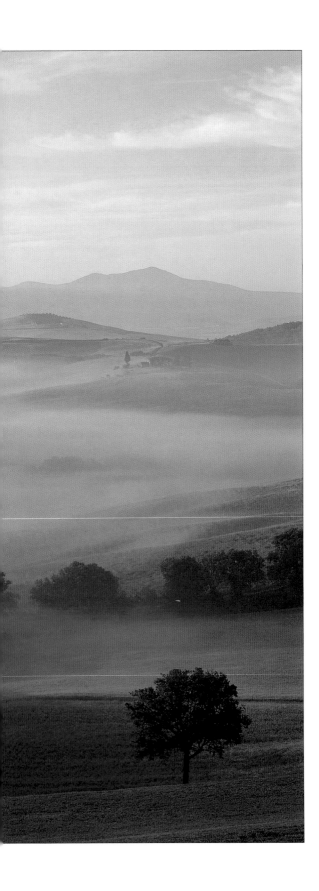

First published in Great Britain in 1999
by Collins & Brown Limited
The Chrysalis Building
Bramley Road
London W10 6SP

A member of **Chrysalis** Books plc

3 5 7 9 8 6 4

British Library Cataloguing-in-Publication Data:
A catalogue record for this book is available from the British Library.

ISBN 1 85585 711 1 (hardback)
ISBN 1 85585 748 0 (paperback)

WRITER: Patricia Monahan

EDITORIAL DIRECTOR: Sarah Hoggett
DESIGNER: Claire Graham
EDITOR: Corinne Asghar

Reproduction by Classic Scan, Singapore
Printed and Bound by Kyodo Printing Co Pte Ltd, Singapore

Front cover: PROVENCE, FRANCE
Back cover: MOUNT FUJI, JAPAN
Page 2: YOSEMITE, USA
Page 3: VERMONT, USA
Page 4–5: TUSCANY, ITALY

CONTENTS

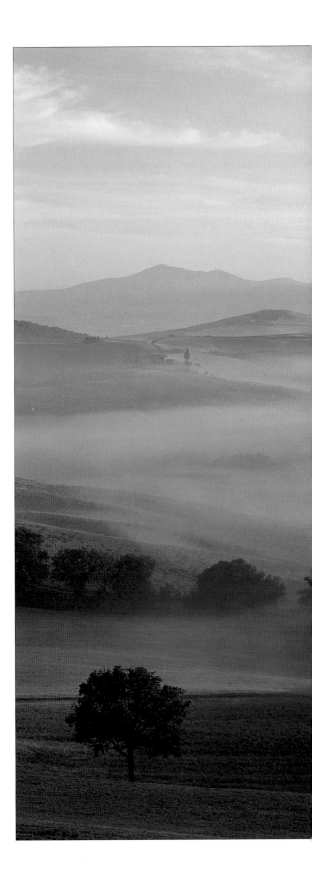

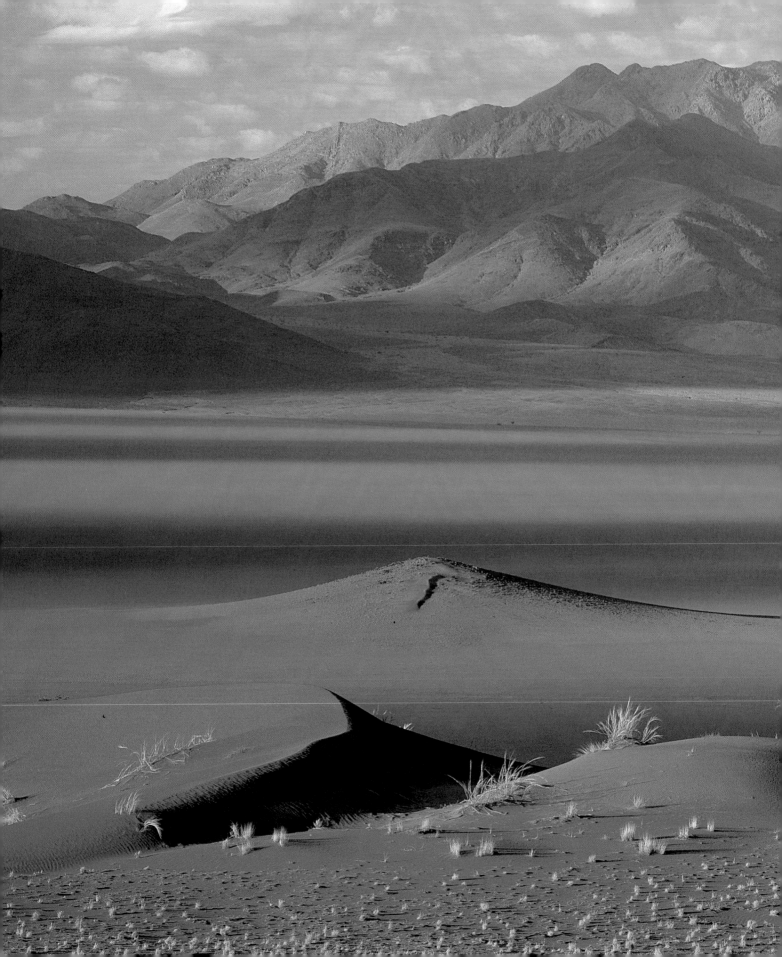

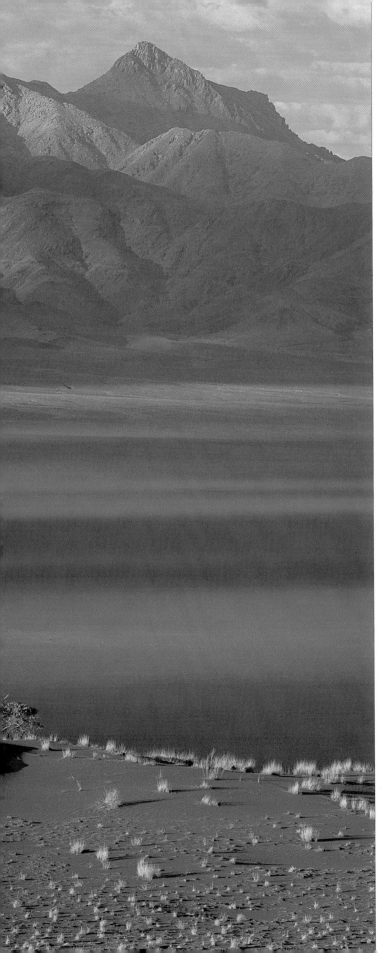

Introduction

THE LANDSCAPE IS fascinating, absorbing, and constantly changing. It changes from day to day, season to season, and often, frustratingly, from one minute to the next. There is always something to enchant, tantalize, and stimulate you, and you will never run out of material. The term 'landscape' encompasses everything from micro landscapes of moss- and lichen-covered boulders, to snow-capped mountains in exotic locations, or sophisticated urban scenes.

The origin of the creative impulse remains unknown. What it is that stimulates the human mind to try to capture a moment, or create an image eludes me. If pressed, I would say that, for me, an intuitive, aesthetic response combines with technical judgement to inspire me to make a photograph. The impulse behind wanting to photograph the landscape must have its origins in the same well of creativity that gives rise to any artistic endeavor. When making a picture I

DAWN LIGHT
The first direct sunlight of dawn produces dense shadows in the foreground. The eye is drawn toward these shadows and then up and through the photograph, via a succession of peaks. Standing in this place, I felt that I was looking at a landscape from the dawn of time.

Location: NAMIBIA, AFRICA

Camera: 6cm x 17cm; Lens: 300mm; Film: Fuji 50 ASA; Exposure: 2 seconds at f.64; Filter: polarizer

7

have to ask myself if it will evoke the essence of the place and of that particular moment. If it does not, then I feel that I will have failed and the photograph will have become nothing more than a mere record.

WHAT MAKES A GOOD LANDSCAPE PHOTOGRAPH?

The landscape is one of the most challenging and rewarding photographic subjects, but a natural landscape rarely conforms to the photographer's ideal – it is often full of untidy bits, fences in the wrong places, and trees that block the view.

When I make a photograph I try to find the underlying order in the landscape – or perhaps, like a gardener, I am trying to impose an order on unruly Nature. I look for simplicity – the graphic lines, shapes, and forms in the landscape. These are the formal qualities that underpin any good work of art, whether it is an opera or a painting. I am trying to 'make' or 'find' an image that is clean and easy to digest. And at the same time I want to capture the magic of the moment, the quality that first drew me to the subject.

The best photographs have a compositional hook – a concept or geometry that provides a solid, underlying structure. Contrasts, similarities, repetitions, symmetries, and asymmetries all occur time and again in my images. There will be sinuous lines – of walls, paths, tree-lined avenues, or waterways – that lead the viewer's eye into the photograph and suggest space, recession, and places beyond the frame. Diagonals have a strong, thrusting energy, and I find 'z'-shapes in the landscape particularly pleasing (see page 120). Often, I deliberately emphasize these

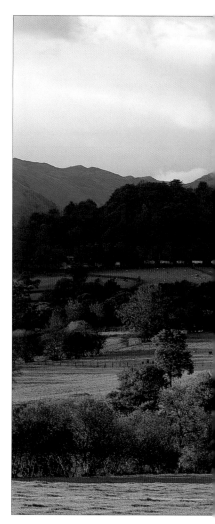

EVENING LIGHT
Barns are one of my favorite subjects and you'll find examples throughout this book. Here a plain but beautifully constructed barn takes the full impact of the evening light on its gable end. It provides an eye-catching focus to which the eye constantly returns.

Location: CUMBRIA, ENGLAND

Camera: 6cm x 6cm;
Lens: 150mm;
Film: Fuji 50 ASA;
Exposure: 1 second at f.32

abstract or decorative qualities, but I try to retain a context, a sense of the landscape from which the image has been taken.

Although a landscape photograph illustrates only a tiny segment of a particular vista, it should be capable of standing alone. All the components should communicate with each other and the image should have an internal logic. Experience and a personal vision tell me what will work, but subconsciously I also run through a checklist of do's and don'ts. So, for example, when I photograph a rural building I see if its shape can be made to echo the slope of

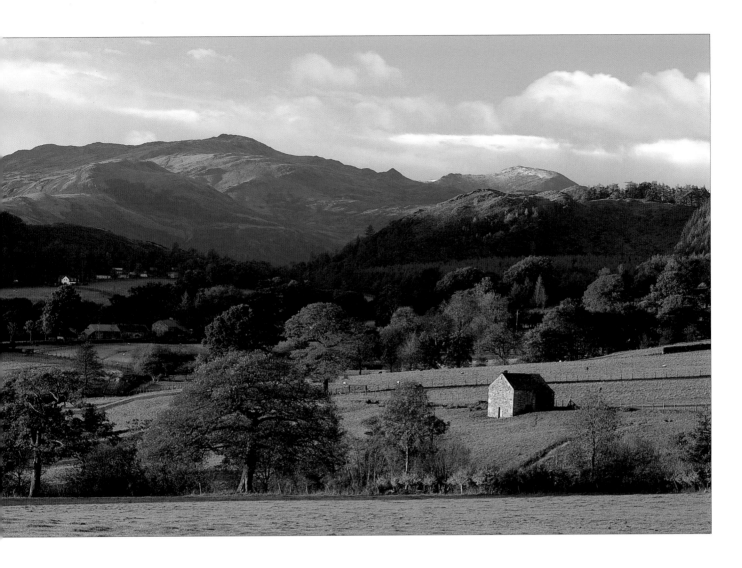

mountains or hills behind. I will often adjust my viewpoint so that a roof is tucked under the skyline and I work hard to ensure that reflections are included in their entirety. If I am photographing an avenue of trees, I will try to make a perfectly symmetrical composition; if not I will create a sweeping diagonal.

The most irritating things in photographs are those that appear arbitrary – the vertical that isn't quite vertical, the spire or tree that just clips the horizon, the shadow that falls nearly-but-not-quite below another feature. Where possible I try to place my main player on a stage or

platform – it creates a focus and a hierarchy that helps the viewer to read the picture.

Inevitably, once the picture has been made I will begin to analyze its content and seek out its meaning. However, I like to think that this is just an unravelling of all that was absorbed spiritually, visually, and intuitively when the photograph was taken. Ultimately the photographer is governed by his or her own personal criteria, or personal taste. These criteria are shaped by a lifetime of experiences and ideals that come together in an instant to make the photograph. Perhaps this very personal act of creation simply stems

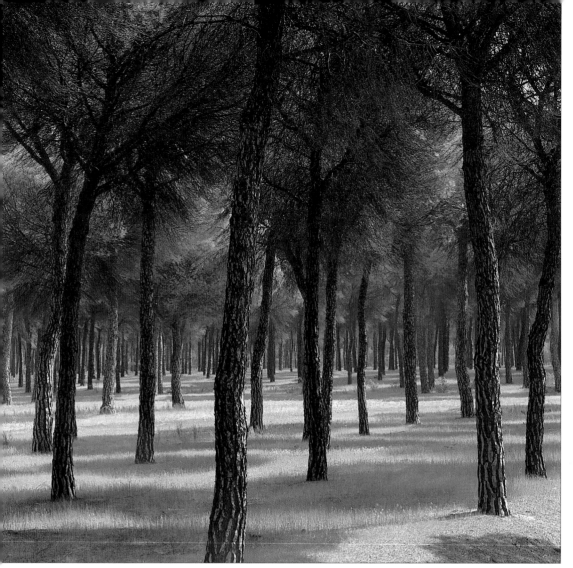

HORIZONTALS AND VERTICALS

The verticals of the woodland are answered by the horizontal shadows, creating a geometry that underpins the pleasing colors and light.

Location: VALLADOLID, SPAIN

Camera: 6cm x 6cm;
Lens: 150mm;
Film: Fuji 50 ASA;
Exposure: ¼ second at f.16–22;
Filter: soft

from a simple wish to glorify those naturally occurring things that seem to us to be beautiful.

COMPOSING A LANDSCAPE PHOTOGRAPH

A photographer 'designs' a picture by selecting, editing, framing, and using light to reveal and conceal elements within the landscape. Wherever possible I do all the composition on the day, through the lens. If I thought I could sort things out later by cropping or manipulating the image, I'd get lazy and the photograph would lose its rigor. It's the limitations, the solving of problems and the pushing of boundaries that give the best results. Your lens is an extension of your eye, and it permits you to select, edit, and frame a 'picture'. Viewpoint is also important. The view from the roadside might be more interesting if seen from close-up, further away, or higher up. So you may have to spend time moving equipment around before you find your picture – but try not to compromise. When the eye is finally pressed against the viewfinder, it begins the next stage of exploration, an initial scan followed by an intense refining process of possible compression, expansion, exclusion, and inclusion. The eye is the photographer's most important tool.

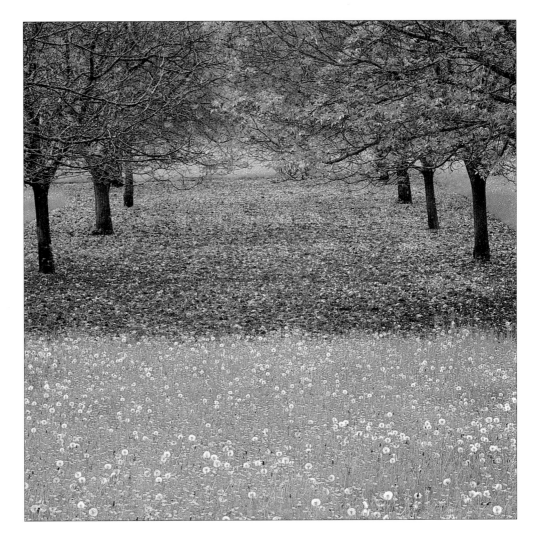

NATURAL FRAME
A centered composition offered an almost perfect symmetry and allowed me to focus on the contrast between the bright, flower-spattered green of the grass in the foreground and the sparkling textures of the pinkish-brown fallen leaves.

Location: DORDOGNE, FRANCE

Camera: 6cm x 6cm;
Lens: 150mm;
Film: Fuji 50 ASA;
Exposure: ⅛ second at f.32;
Filter: 81A (warm up)

Trying to find a perfect and complete pattern can be frustrating – but the sense of triumph when it works is worth it. If you do not have a perspective control lens or a camera with movements, a step ladder is useful for photographing tall subjects like trees, and tall buildings as these tend to converge above your eye level. By raising yourself above the ground you can reduce these distortions – if I hadn't used a ladder for the poplar study on page 81, the trees would have converged. A ladder is also useful for overhead photographs, but sometimes it simply allows me to see further and include a whole shadow or reflection.

LIGHT ON THE LANDSCAPE
Light is the most important element in any landscape photograph – not only does it set the mood, dictate the character of the shadows, and affect the color and tonal relationships, it can also be used to hide untidy or unimportant features, and highlight those that are important. I have waited for hours for the sun and clouds to do what I want them to do (see pages 112–113) but at other times the changes occur at breakneck speed (see pages 48–49). With experience you acquire a better understanding of weather and light so that you can predict, to some extent, what will happen.

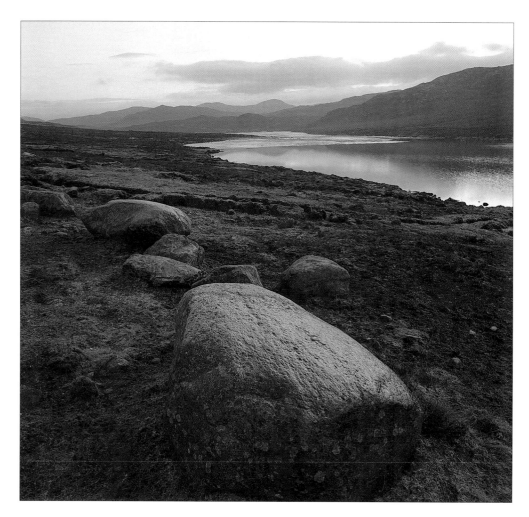

LEADING THE EYE: 1
The granite boulders emphasize the foreground plane while the crisply defined and overlapping hills create a sense of space and recession. The eye dances from the light on the pitted granite to the glassy surface of the loch and on to the silvery sky in the distance.

Location: WESTERN ISLES, SCOTLAND

Camera: 6cm x 6cm;
Lens: 50mm;
Film: Fuji 100 ASA;
Exposure: ¼ second at f.32

The transitional times and the two transitional seasons often produce the most pleasing light effects. The landscape photographer feeds on this variety. Like a painter, my favorite times are early morning and late afternoon and evening, although you have to be on your toes to capture the fleeting effects, and to decide which is the perfect moment. Apart from during the winter, the light at midday can be harsh and unflattering. The effect is a bit like that created by the center light in a room, where the harsh, top light does nothing to enhance the mood.

SKY, CLOUDS, OR NO SKY
The sky is the source of the light and weather in the landscape, and can really set the mood. A good sky can make a photograph, while a poor one can make a potentially good photograph merely mediocre. I'll crop out a dazzling blue sky if it conflicts with the color balance of the rest of the image, and I'll sometimes eliminate the sky in order to create a more contained mood – to focus attention on something in the landscape below or to deliberately create a flatter, more abstract image. Cloud forms are infinitely varied

LEADING THE EYE: 2

The repeating planes and geometries of walls and roofs combine the simplicity of an abstract pattern with the complexity of a Cubist painting.

Location: ANDALUSIA, SPAIN

Camera: 6cm x 6cm;
Lens: 80mm;
Film: Fuji 100 ASA;
Exposure: ⅟₁₅ second at f.16–22
Filter: polarizer

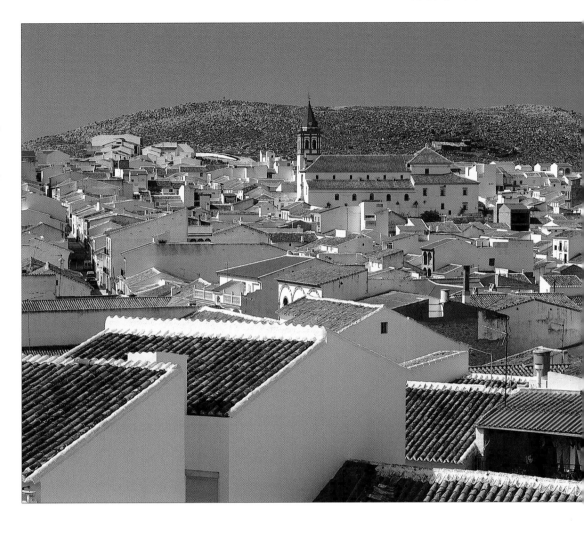

and fascinating, and I've waited patiently for hours for clouds to arrive just where I want them (see page 37). Perhaps one-third or four-fifths of a landscape will be devoted to sky. How envious I am of the painter who will see the poverty of a prevailing sky and simply conjure up a sky of his or her own choosing. Sometimes the sky simply begs to be photographed – in the photograph on page 50, I noticed the sky first and then I had to look for something to go with it!

Landscape photography is about so many things – choosing the right location, the correct equipment for the job, capturing the essence of the image – but primarily photographing the landscape should give you pleasure. There really is nothing like the feeling when the light, the color, shapes, balance, and all the components interlock so perfectly that you feel overwhelmed by the wonder of it. It is a fulfilling act of creation that tells you and the viewer as much about yourself as about the actual landscape. But ultimately, as I hope I have conveyed through these photographs, landscape photography is all about perception, it is about 'seeing'.

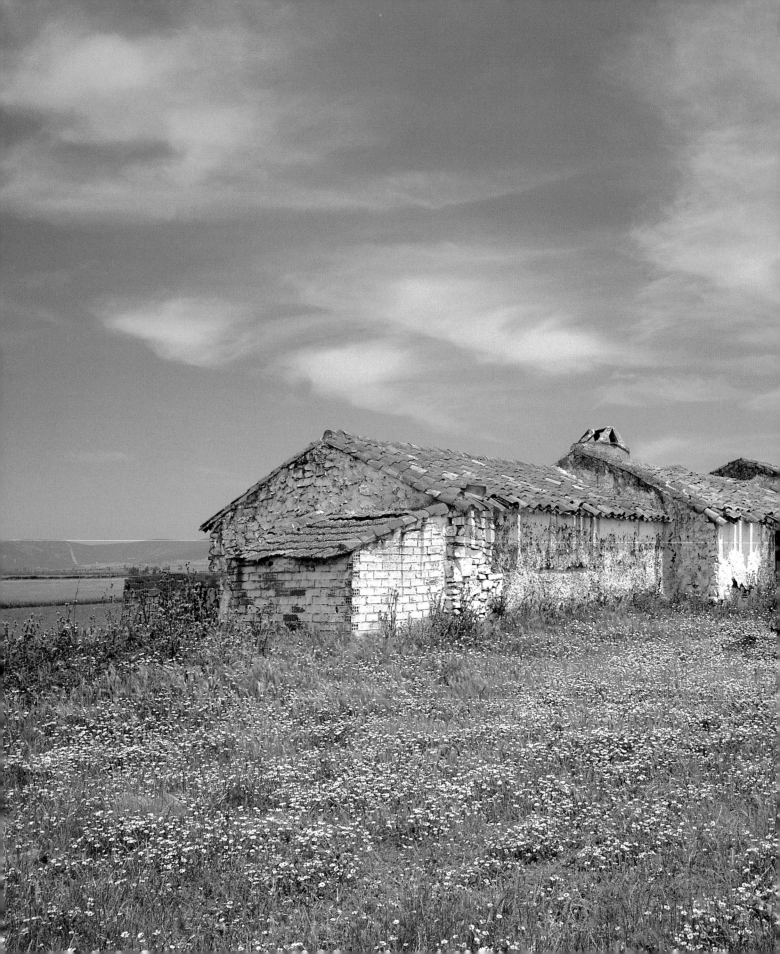

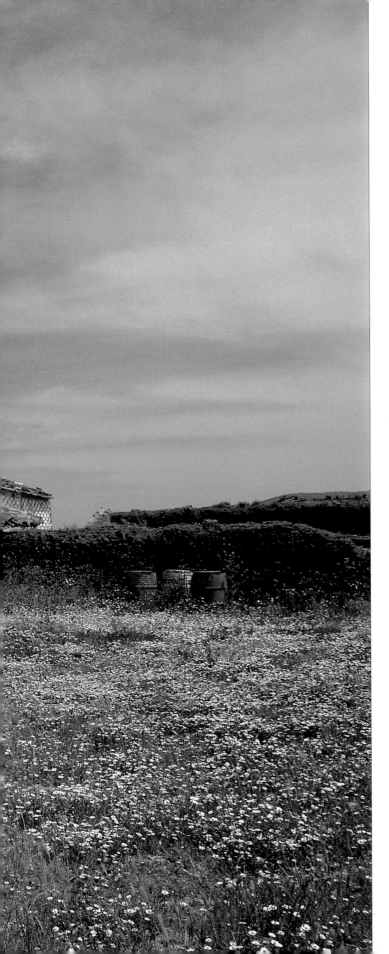

Qualities of the Photograph

Color, texture, and pattern are important themes for the landscape photographer, but it is primarily light that dictates the mood, and even the appearance, of a picture. Early morning and evening offer the most glorious light, while spring and fall are the most pictorially rewarding times of the year.

SPRINGTIME IN ANDALUSIA

My eye was caught by the way the roofs of these humble buildings cascade down the hillside, hugging its gentle contours. The carpet of spring flowers echoes the color of the rough, whitewashed walls and the texture of the pantiled roofs. Everything seemed to harmonize beautifully – even the sky had a wispy, light-hearted feeling. I did try to move the barrels, but they were full of water, and in the end they were not too distracting.

Location: CIUDAD REAL, SPAIN

Camera: 6cm x 6cm; Lens: 50mm; Film: Kodak 64 ASA; Exposure: 1 second at f.16; Filter: polarizer

15

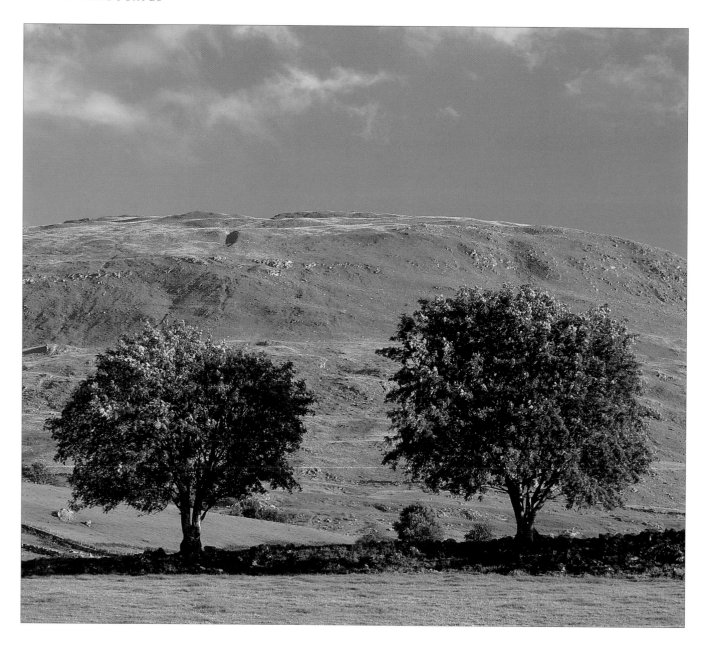

TWO TREES, FOREGROUND

A pair of rowan trees stands guarding a hillside in Scotland. The raking light glances
across the hillside, giving it the appearance of brushed suede. The light sparkles on granite
boulders and the domes of the trees, and throws the trees and bank into stark silhouette.

Location: THE BORDERS, SCOTLAND

Camera: 6cm x 6cm; Lens: 150mm; Film: Fuji 50 ASA;
Exposure: $\frac{1}{15}$ second at f.16; Filter: polarizer

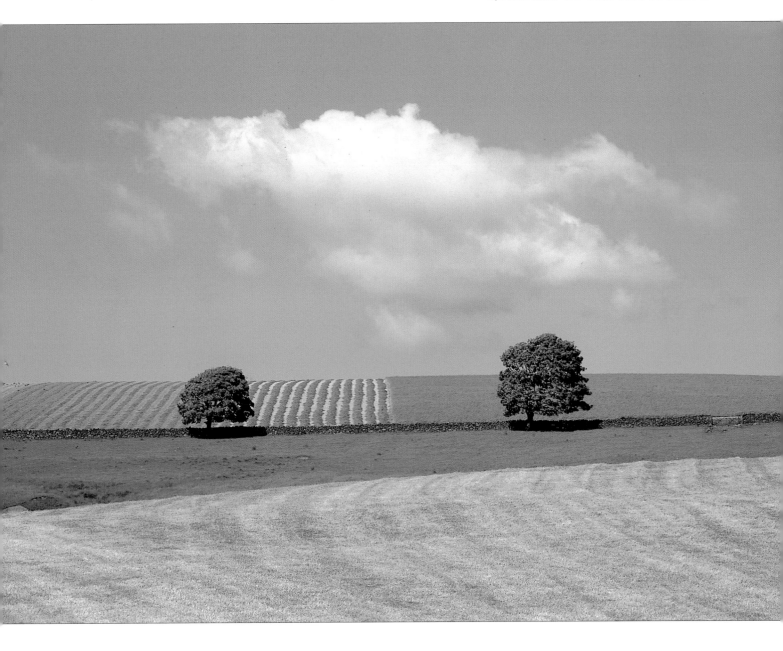

TWO TREES, MIDDLE DISTANCE

Once again two symmetrically placed trees are the subject of the photograph, but this time the pared-down geometry of the landscape creates an entirely different mood. The clouds dangling like a canopy over the hill give the photograph a surreal quality.

Location: THE BORDERS, SCOTLAND

Camera: 6cm x 6cm; Lens: 150mm; Film: Kodak 64 ASA;
Exposure: ¼ second at f.22–32; Filter: polarizer

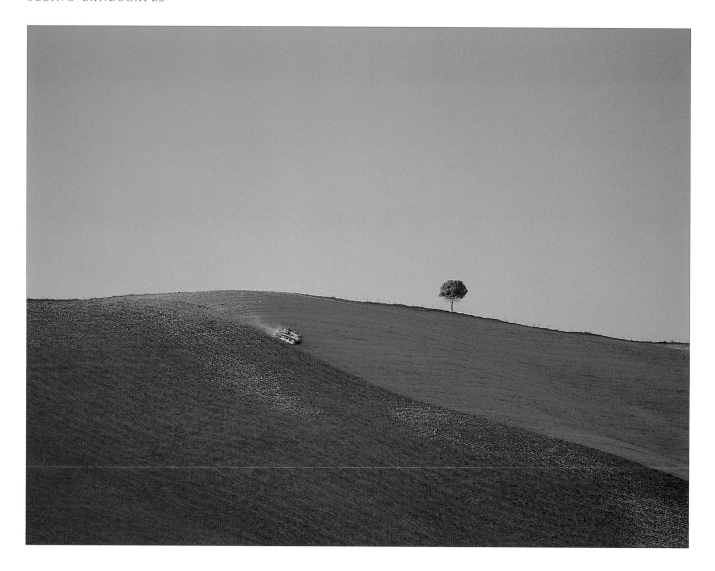

CLASSIC POSITIONING

This subject is simple – a tractor, a field, a tree, and an expanse of sky – and the composition is bold. The horizon is almost on the half-way split, while the single tree isolated on the hilltop marks the one-third division of the frame. The earthy browns are in perfect harmony with the clear blue sky, and the yellow tractor provides a bright spot of color.

Location: TUSCANY, ITALY

Camera: 6cm x 6cm; Lens: 150mm; Film: Fuji 100 ASA;
Exposure: 1/30 second at f.11; Filter: polarizer

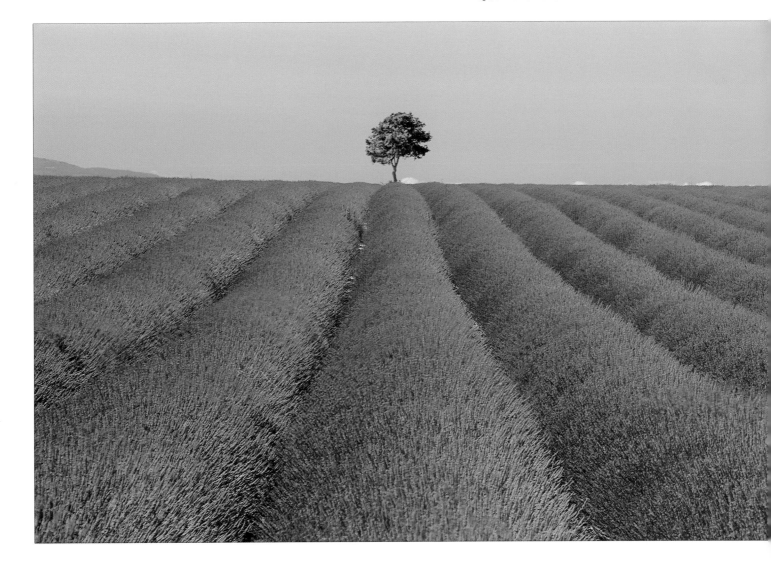

BARE ESSENTIALS

The simplest solutions are often the best. I go to great lengths to strip away anything but the bare essentials to find the simplicity that underlies the landscape. The high skyline, the symmetrical banks of lavender receding toward the horizon, and the single centrally placed tree combine to make a dramatic composition.

Location: PROVENCE, FRANCE

Camera: 35mm; Lens: 105mm; Film: Fuji 100 ASA;
Exposure: ⅛ second at f.22; Filter: polarizer

19

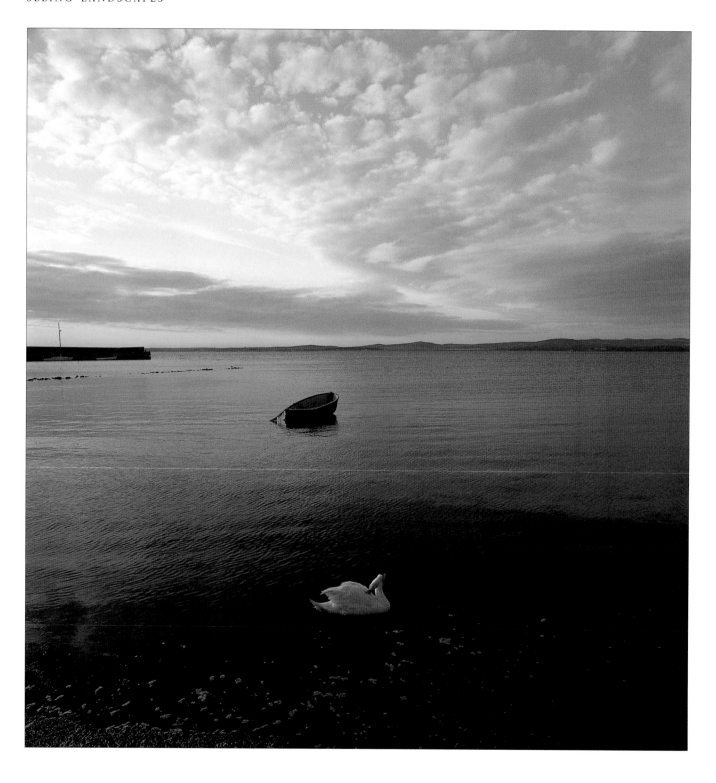

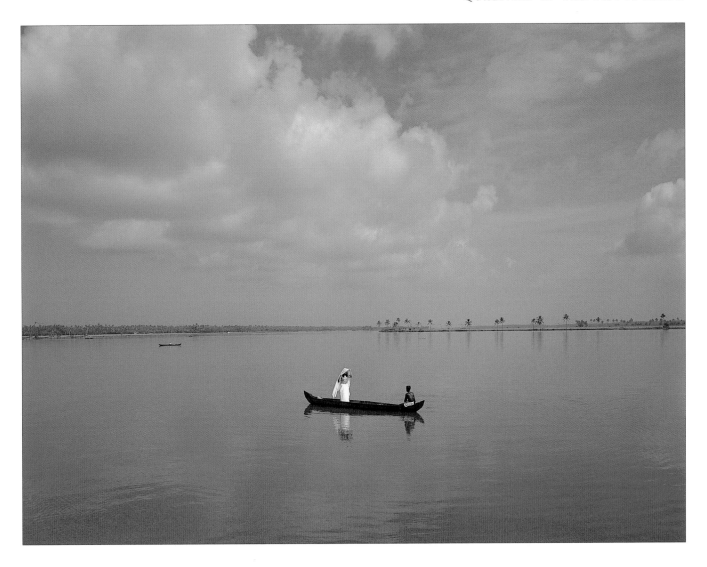

USING DIAGONALS

The fleeting pageant of the evening sky over water offers infinite possibilities, but to avoid clichés the picture must be carefully constructed. The clouds funneling toward the horizon, the shadow's edge on the water, and the moored boat are all aligned along diagonals that give the image an internal dynamic. The swan was a bonus – it drifted into the shadow where its plumage echoed the clouds above.

Location: WESTERN ISLES, SCOTLAND

Camera: 6cm x 6cm; Lens: 50mm; Film: Fuji 100 ASA; Exposure: ¹⁄₁₅ second at f.16–22; Filter: polarizer

ABSTRACT SIMPLICITY

Water and sky provide endless scope for 'picture-making'. Here their muted tones provide a wonderful foil for the charcoal-dark, arrow-like canoe, and the standing figure in her dazzling white drapery. This single, emphatic focal point in a large field has an abstract simplicity. I have deliberately placed the focus center stage and about one-third from the bottom edge.

Location: KERALA, INDIA

Camera: 6cm x 6cm; Lens: 50mm; Film: Fuji 100 ASA; Exposure: ¹⁄₆₀ second at f.8; Filter: polarizer

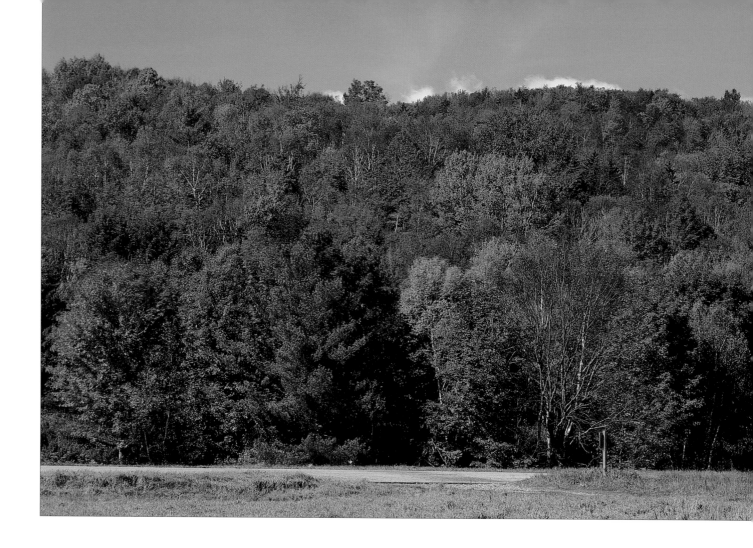

EDITING THE IMAGE

I just loved this dilapidated little barn with its jaunty air and its doors falling off their hinges. I was particularly captivated by the textures of the peeling red paint on the clapboard and the way they are picked up and echoed by the richly colored foliage behind. The small square windows are reminiscent of eyes and everything is neatly outlined in white paint. When I introduced myself to the owner the day before, he couldn't believe that I wanted to photograph the barn – he was thinking of pulling it down. Much to his surprise an American photographer had already taken a picture, which is hanging on a senator's wall in Washington.

I prefer the cropped version of the photograph. It loses the blue of the sky, which is a distraction because there is no blue anywhere else. The road on the left is intrusive in a picture that is really about decay and times past, and because it is pale in color your eye ricochets backward and forward between path and barn. The cropped version is much calmer and concentrates on the little barn.

Location: VERMONT, USA

Camera: 6cm x 17cm; Lens: 300mm; Film: Fuji 50 ASA; Exposure: 1 second at f.45; Filter: polarizer

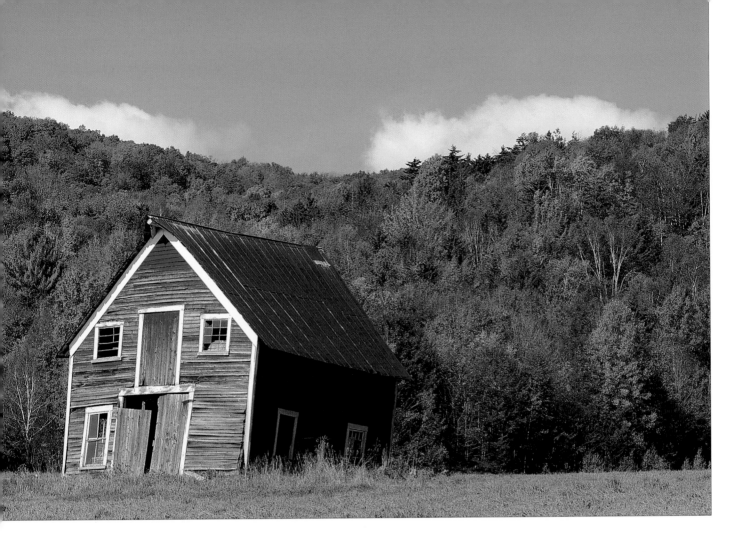

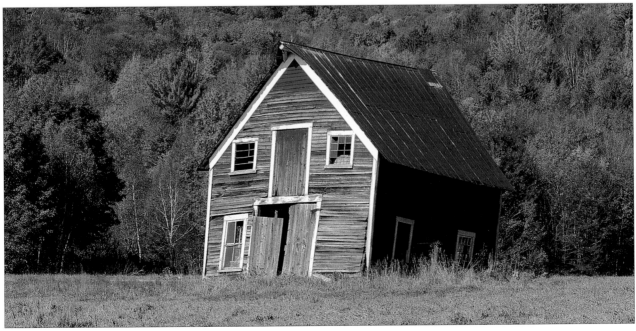

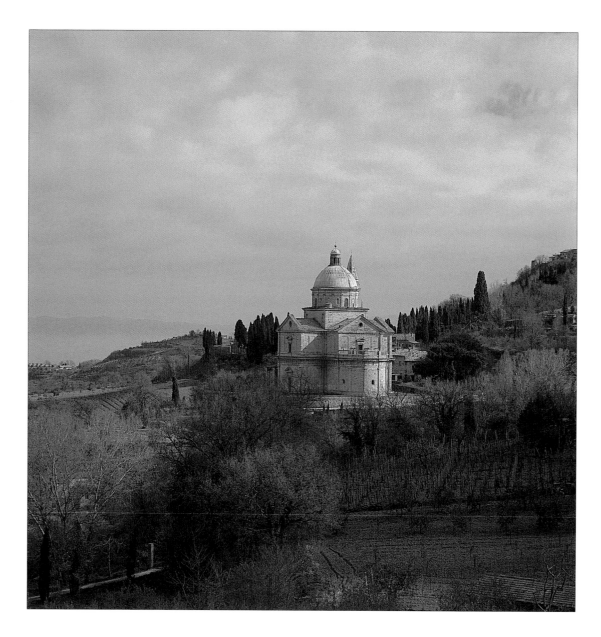

MONTEPULCIANO, MORNING

The appearance of the landscape changes dramatically throughout the day, so you must decide when your subject will be shown at its best. Here, morning light casts crisp, dark shadows on the walls of the basilica, revealing the fine articulations of pilasters and capitals, while the shaded side and the trees in the foreground are shrouded in transparent shadow. Compare this with the entirely different mood achieved by evening light.

Location: TUSCANY, ITALY

Camera: 6cm x 6cm; Lens: 150mm; Film: Fuji 100 ASA;
Exposure: ½ second at f.22; Filters: polarizer, 81A (warm up)

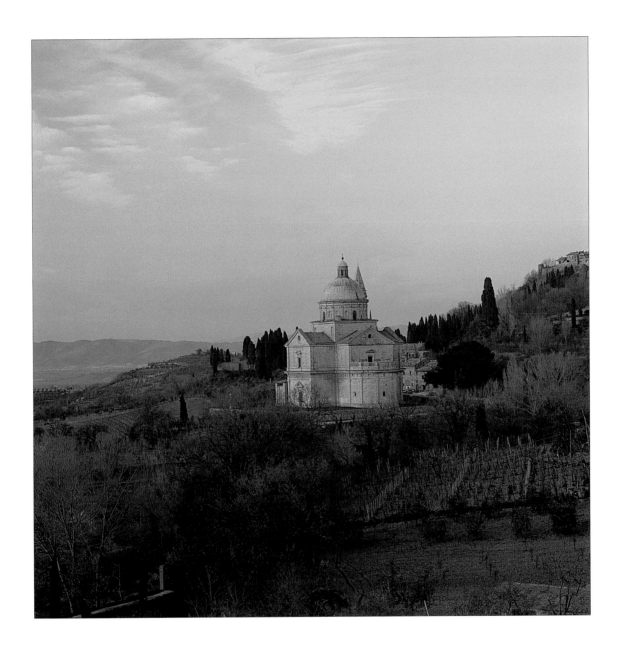

MONTEPULCIANO, EVENING

The afterglow that envelops the landscape just as the sun goes down has a truly magical quality. The sun seems to have disappeared, and just when you think it is all over something rather miraculous happens. There is no direct light, but the setting sun reflecting off the underside of the clouds bathes the landscape in a softly translucent light that is almost tactile. The moment lasts only three or four minutes, so you must be ready.

Location: TUSCANY, ITALY

Camera: 6cm x 6cm; Lens: 150mm; Film: Fuji 100 ASA;
Exposure: ½ second at f.22; Filters: polarizer, 81B (warm up)

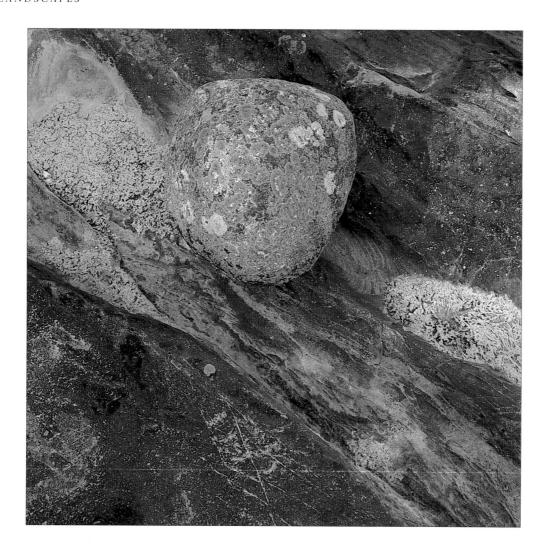

LICHEN AND ROCK

The intimacies of the landscape have plenty to offer, so when you are looking for pictures don't neglect what is beneath your feet. Here veined bedrock and a lichen-encrusted boulder have an abstract quality. A palette of golds, silvers, and grays combined with dappled patterns creates a decorative surface, while the ambiguities of scale allow the mind to see strange and mysterious landscapes.

Location: WESTERN ISLES, SCOTLAND

Camera: 6cm x 6cm; Lens: 50mm;
Film: Fuji 50 ASA; Exposure: ½ second at f.22

SCULPTED ROCK

Swirling, gouged, and eroded rocks provide a glimpse of the forces of nature that made this landscape. The photograph provides visual entertainment, but like all good images it makes you look again and ask: what is it and how did it come to be like this? If a picture does that I feel it has worked. The clump of plants give a clue to scale, so this image is less abstract than that on the facing page.

Location: WESTERN ISLES, SCOTLAND

Camera: 6cm x 6cm; Lens: 50mm;
Film: Fuji 50 ASA; Exposure: ¼ second at f.22

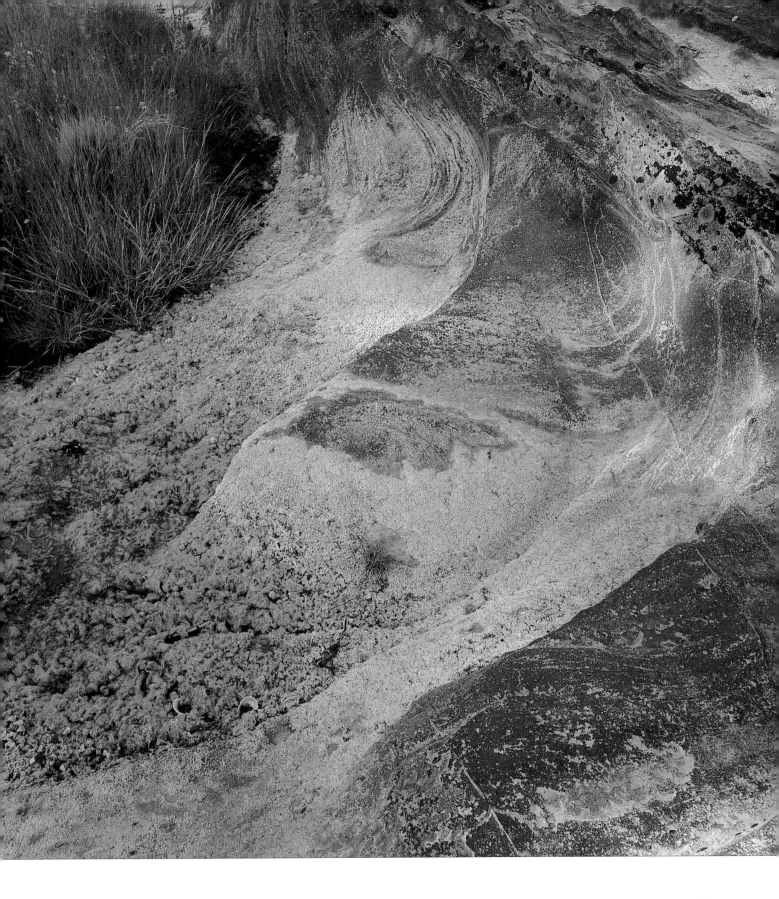

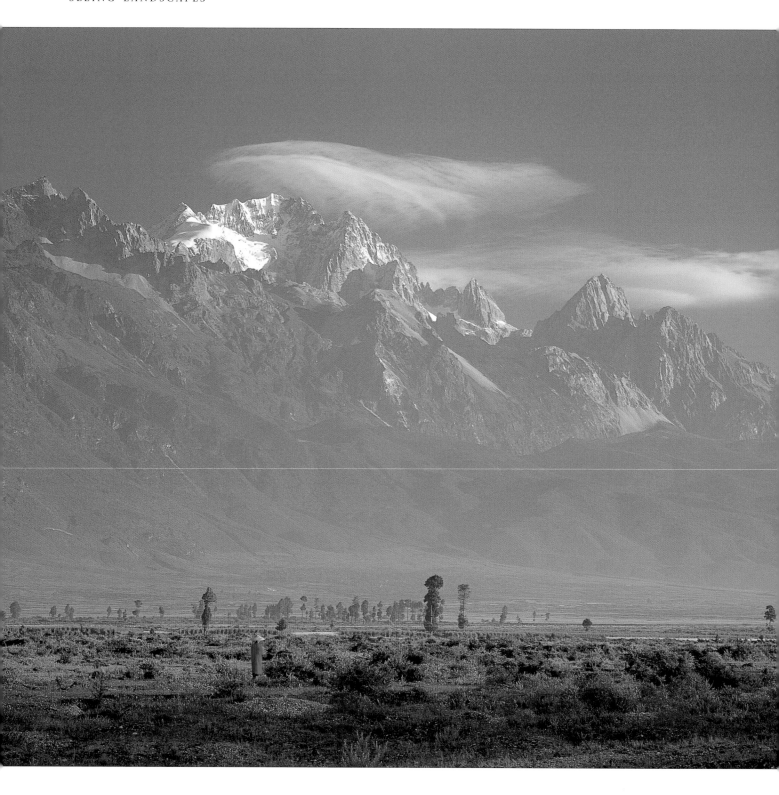

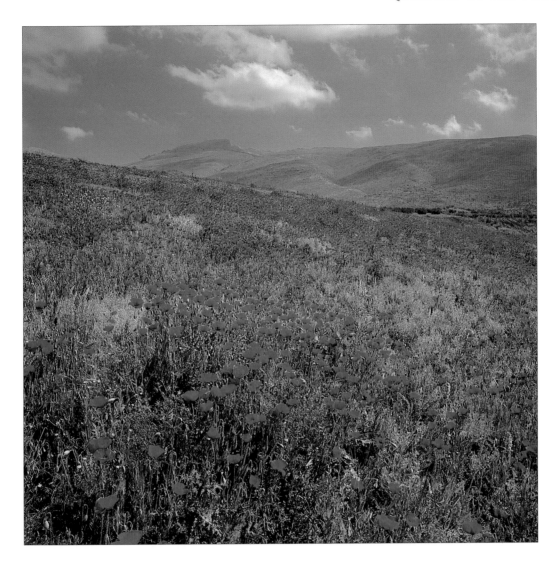

A SENSE OF SCALE

On five occasions, the mountain was shrouded in cloud but on the sixth day it was clear, so at 5:30 AM we drove to the site. The sun was coming up fast, and shadows raced across the landscape. Our driver was persuaded to wear the hat and jacket and to walk into the landscape to provide a color splash and a sense of scale. Red is such an insistent color that even a tiny area can transform an image.

Location: LIJIANG, CHINA

Camera: 6cm x 6cm; Lens: 150mm;
Film: Fuji 100 ASA; Exposure: ⅕ second at f.22

PROFUSION OF COLOR

There is nothing quite as thrilling as sitting among a mass of wild flowers, and the photographic potential is obvious. It is important that there is an abundance of color – half measures will not do. I would have preferred a solid mass of red, but red and green do resonate against each other – so the poppies in the center of the image positively pulsate.

Location: ANDALUSIA, SPAIN

Camera: 6cm x 6cm; Lens: 50mm; Film: Fuji 50 ASA; Exposure: ¼ second at f.22–32; Filter: polarizer

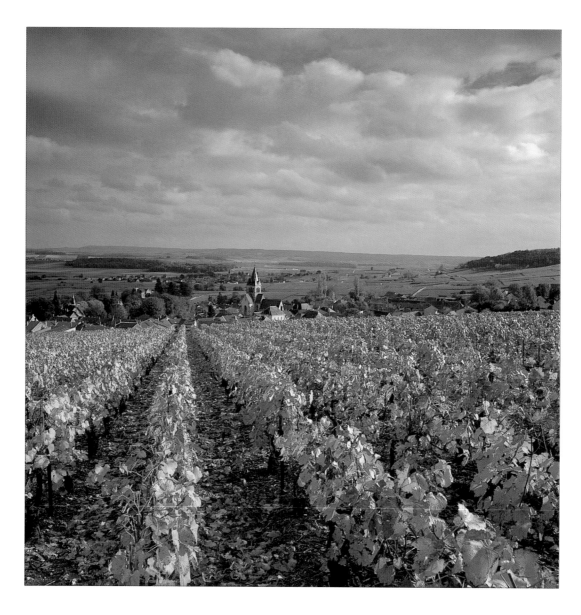

VINES IN A LANDSCAPE

This was my first attempt to photograph this scene, but it didn't take me long to realize that a more abstract version would work better. The eye is drawn toward the horizon but the church is too small to provide a focus. The ground between the vines is colorful and richly textured, but it is far too dominant. The rain-filled sky imparts a pleasing softness to the scene, but visually it doesn't relate to the vines and the landscape below. While this might work as a topographical study, I find the simplicity of the other version more intriguing.

Location: NEAR ÉPERNAY, FRANCE

Camera: 6cm x 6cm; Lens: 50mm; Film: Fuji 50 ASA;
Exposure: ¼ second at f.22–32; Filters: low-density, graduated

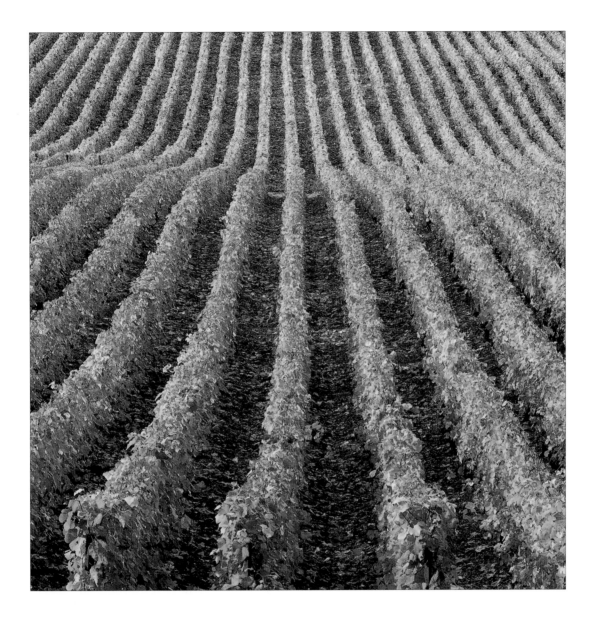

ABSTRACTED VINEYARD

Recession in the landscape is always a good basis for a composition. These vines create a bold, graphic motif as they work their way up the hillside, following the undulations of the landscape. The colors of the foliage sparkle in the sunlight, while the rows between the vines are dappled with shadows, creating a rich mix of color and texture. I opted for a high viewpoint so that I could fill the frame with vines. I moved my ladder until I found a position that gave me a symmetrical arrangement of rows converging toward the top center of the image.

Location: NEAR ÉPERNAY, FRANCE

Camera: 6cm x 6cm; Lens: 150mm;
Film: Fuji 50 ASA; Exposure: ⅛ second at f.16

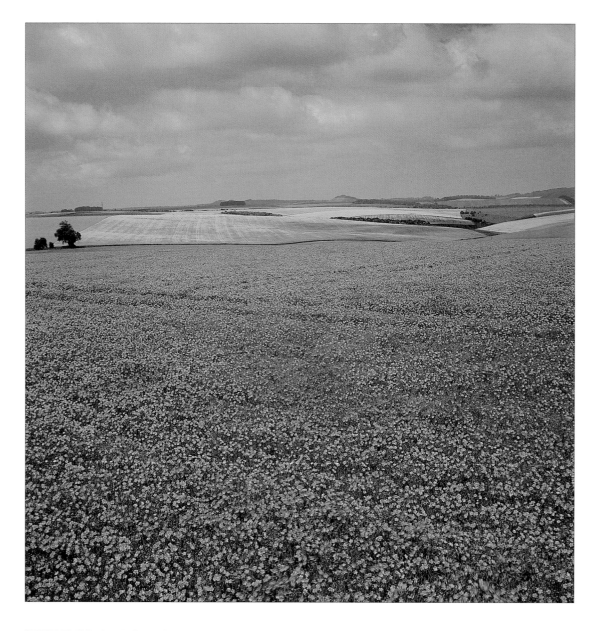

STUDY IN YELLOW AND LILAC: 1

The blue-violet of linseed is amazingly difficult to photograph. On the other side of the field the color disappears as the light is scattered from the tiny petals. These pictures were taken within 20 minutes of each other. Here, the yellow advances. You get a spatial distortion that makes it appear more flat and abstract.

Location: WILTSHIRE, ENGLAND

Camera: 6cm x 6cm; Lens: 50mm; Film: Fuji 50 ASA;
Exposure: ¼ second at f.22–32; Filters: polarizer, low-density, graduated

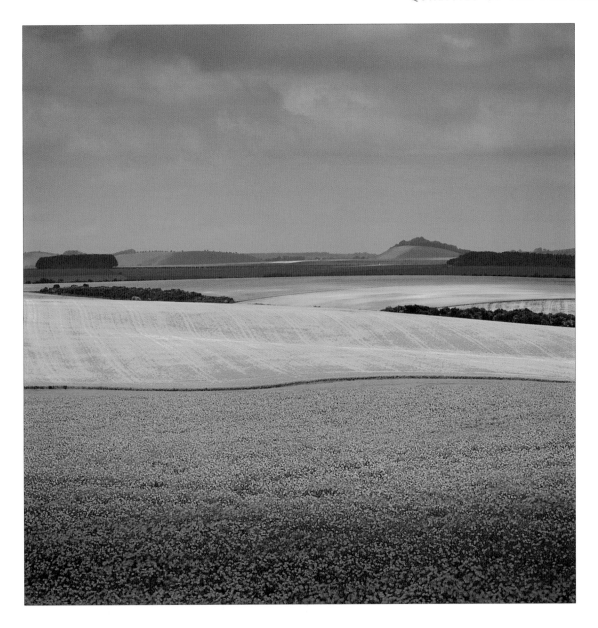

STUDY IN YELLOW AND LILAC: 2

I took this picture first, but I found the yellow too overwhelming. To achieve the right effect the flowers needed to be caught at the right time and from the right angle. I was looking for a balance between the two. A little yellow goes a long way – for harmony you need less yellow and more lilac.

Location: WILTSHIRE, ENGLAND

Camera: 6cm x 6cm; Lens: 150mm; Film: Fuji 50 ASA;
Exposure: ¼ second at f.22; Filter: low-density, graduated

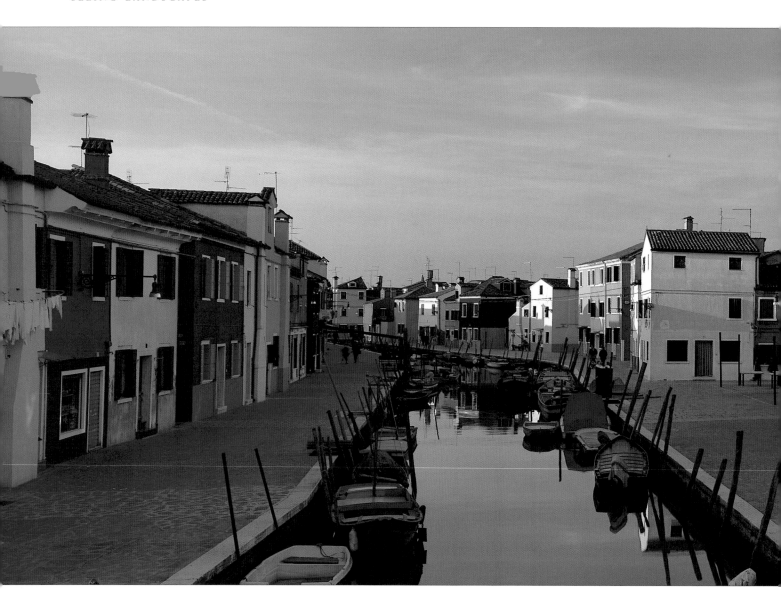

LIGHT AND COLOR

This picture is about light, but it is only 30% lit. On the left of the canal there is no direct light, while the right is in the shadow of the facing buildings. The reflective qualities of the sky and water mean that even shaded areas are lively. Some of the facades on the right receive bright light, and you are drawn to the flickers of light where the canal curves away. The pink facade at that point looks especially vibrant because it is surrounded by dark tones.

Location: VENICE, ITALY

Camera: 6cm x 17cm; Lens: 105mm; Film: Fuji 100 ASA;
Exposure: ¼ second at f.45; Filter: polarizer

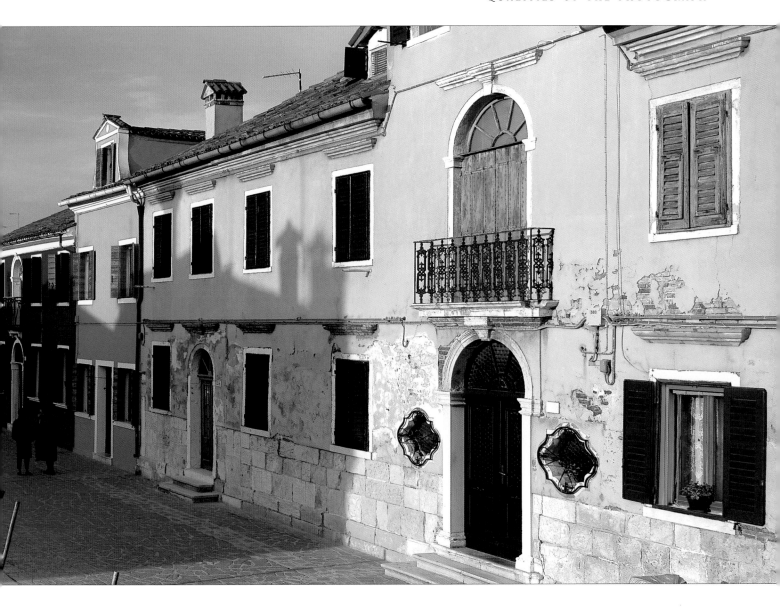

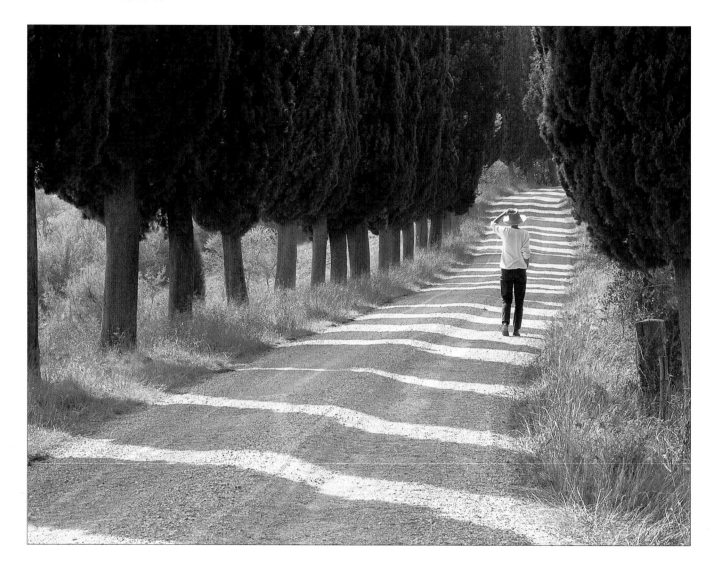

LIGHT AND SHADE

The road leads you into the picture, while the columnar trunks of the trees and the bands of shadow provide a sense of pace and recession. The dense foliage contains the picture and creates a spare and compact composition. I have a version of this with no figure, but the shadows aren't as emphatic. I think I would have preferred to have no person, but to retain strong shadows.

Location: TUSCANY, ITALY

Camera: 35mm; Lens: 135mm;
Film: Fuji 50 ASA; Exposure: ¼ second at f.22

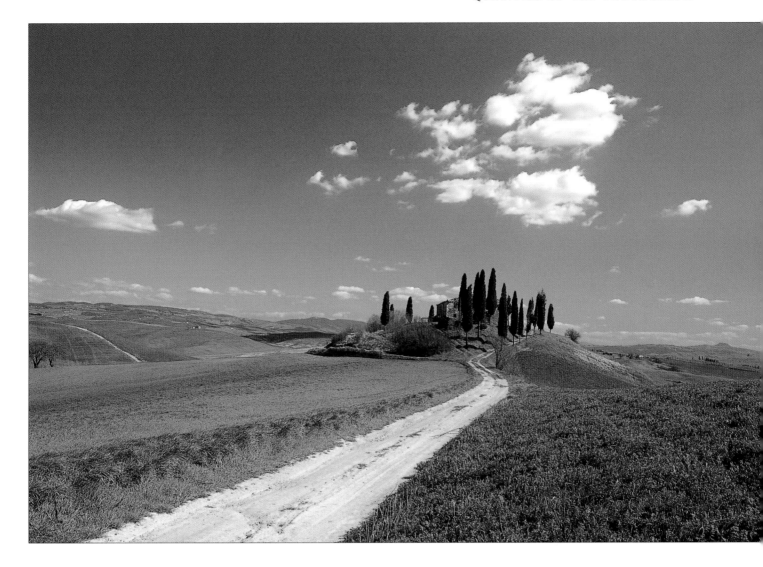

SWEEPING DIAGONAL

Again, a diagonal line sweeps into the picture, drawing the eye
to the Tuscan hilltop farmhouse with its palisade of cypresses. I
had to wait a while to catch the flurry of clouds at just this point,
but it was worth it because they provide a humorous punctuation
and give the sky a sense of recession.

Location: TUSCANY, ITALY

Camera: 35mm; Lens: 28mm; Film: Fuji 100 ASA;
Exposure: ⅛ second at f.22; Filter: polarizer

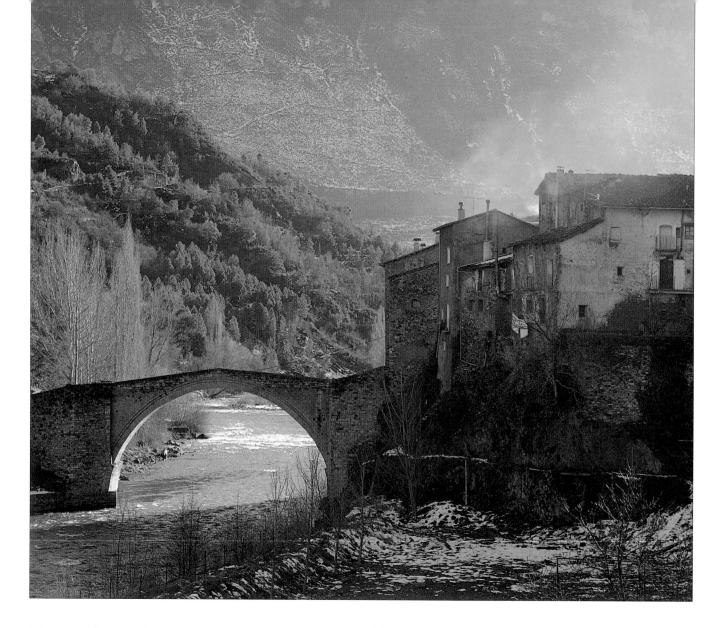

BACKLIT BRIDGE

Inevitably and inexorably the eye is drawn to the brightest part of the picture – the water framed by the graceful stone bridge. Backlighting creates an inside-outside feeling. On this side of the bridge everything is in shadow so that the cascading buildings meld with the bridge to create an emphatic silhouette. The landscape is bathed in a warm, hazy light that gives it an ethereal look. Smoke rising from a hidden fire takes on a pinkish hue.

Location: Lérida, Spain

Camera: 6cm x 6cm; Lens: 150mm; Film: Fuji 50 ASA; Exposure: ⅛ second at f.16; Filter: 81B (warm up)

CAPTURING THE MOOD

This abandoned village covered in evening light has a strange, eerie quality. Its windows are black and devoid of glass, there are no electricity wires, no television aerials. The blue sky and the warm light contrast with the unsettling and somber mood of the picture – but the dark, looming curtain of rock behind has a brooding feel. There are two separate stories told in a single picture.

Location: Navarre, Spain

Camera: 6cm x 6cm; Lens: 150mm; Film: Fuji 50 ASA; Exposure: 1/15 second at f.11–16; Filter: 81B (warm up)

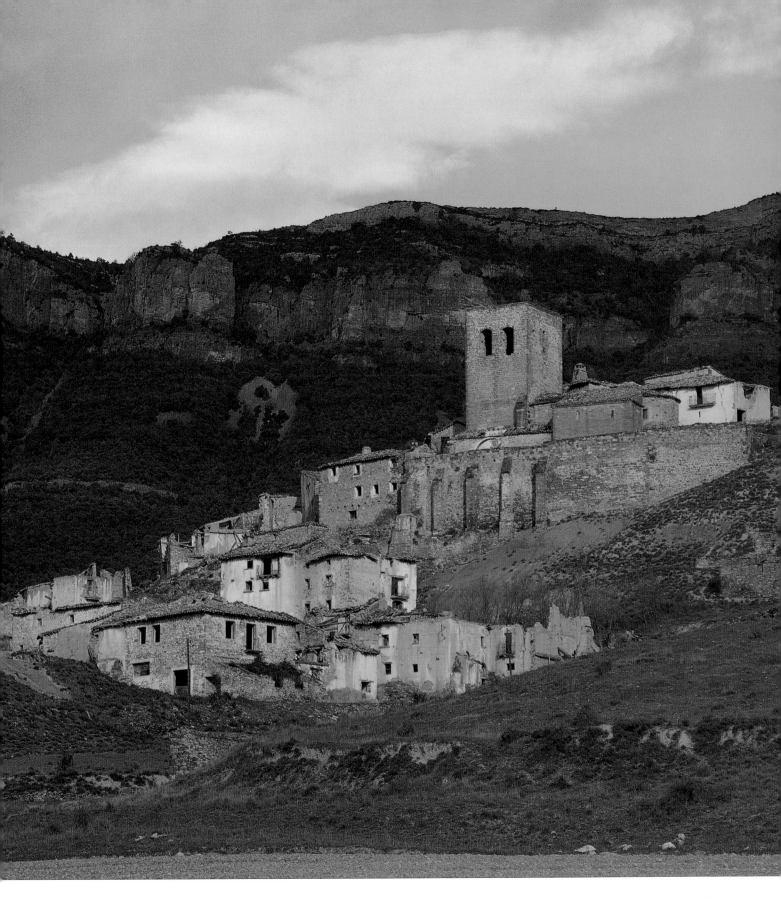

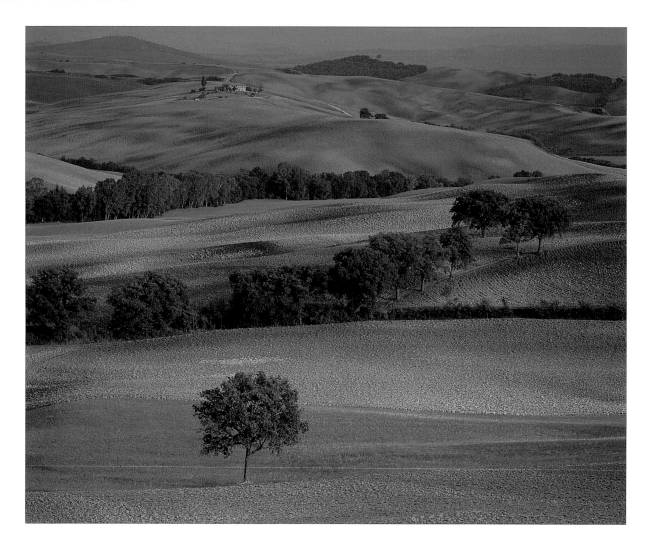

TEXTURED LANDSCAPE

The oblique late-afternoon light picks up the texture of the earth and the ridges left by a harrow. The uneven terrain in this area resembles a lumpy mattress. The tones are predominantly muted and earthy, with the green trees and the emerging wheat providing a starkly contrasting pattern. The single tree at the bottom provides a lead-in and links to the trees along the track. It is a picture in which the eye can wander.

Location: TUSCANY, ITALY

Camera: 6cm x 6cm; Lens: 150mm; Film: Fuji 50 ASA;
Exposure: ½ second at f.32; Filters: polarizer, 81B (warm up)

A SWITCH-BACK ROAD

The pleasing, sinuous line of a road, a stream, or a wall provides a graceful lead-in to a photograph. My high viewpoint allowed me to see the road snaking up the hill and I have cropped in tightly so that the road occupies the center of the picture. I like the contrast between the velvety columns of the cypress trees and the dusty soil. The strength of this image lies in the upper part.

Location: TUSCANY, ITALY

Camera: 6cm x 6cm; Lens: 250mm; Film: Fuji 100 ASA;
Exposure: ⅕ second at f.11–16;
Filters: polarizer, 81A (warm up)

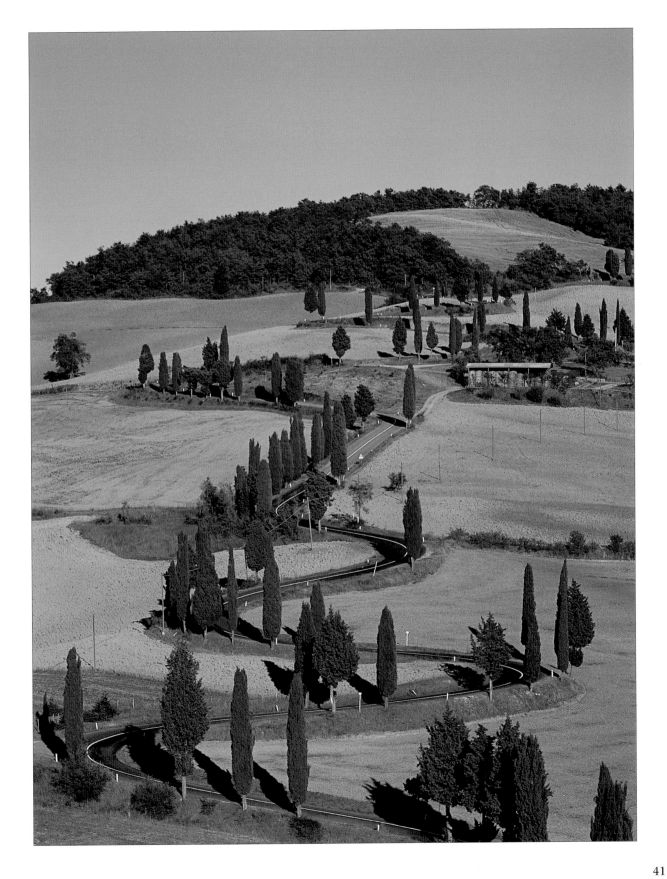

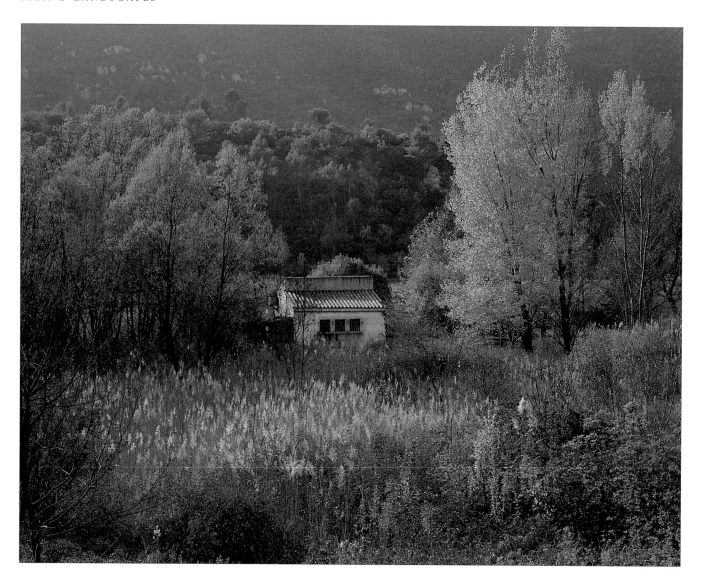

GLORIOUS COLOR

I have a passion for reeds, especially after the summer when the golds, creams, and beiges recall the colors of a tapestry. Light slanting in from one side picked out their textures and illuminated the foliage on the tree on the right, while the gray hill behind provided the right neutral foil. The pumping station creates a focus.

Location: PROVENCE, FRANCE

Camera: 6cm x 6cm; Lens: 80mm; Film: Kodak 64 ASA; Exposure: ⅛ second at f.22; Filter: polarizer

GOLDEN HARMONY

I must admit that someone else spotted this scene, but I found the image utterly compelling. I liked the emphatic flecks of the pumpkin stems, the density of the tree trunk, the almost-black branches snaking through the gilded canopy, and the way the tree foliage echoed the pumpkin colors. A warm filter enhanced the mood.

Location: VERMONT, USA

Camera: 6cm x 6cm; Lens: 150mm; Film: Fuji 100 ASA; Exposure: ¼ second at f.22–32; Filter: 81C (warm up)

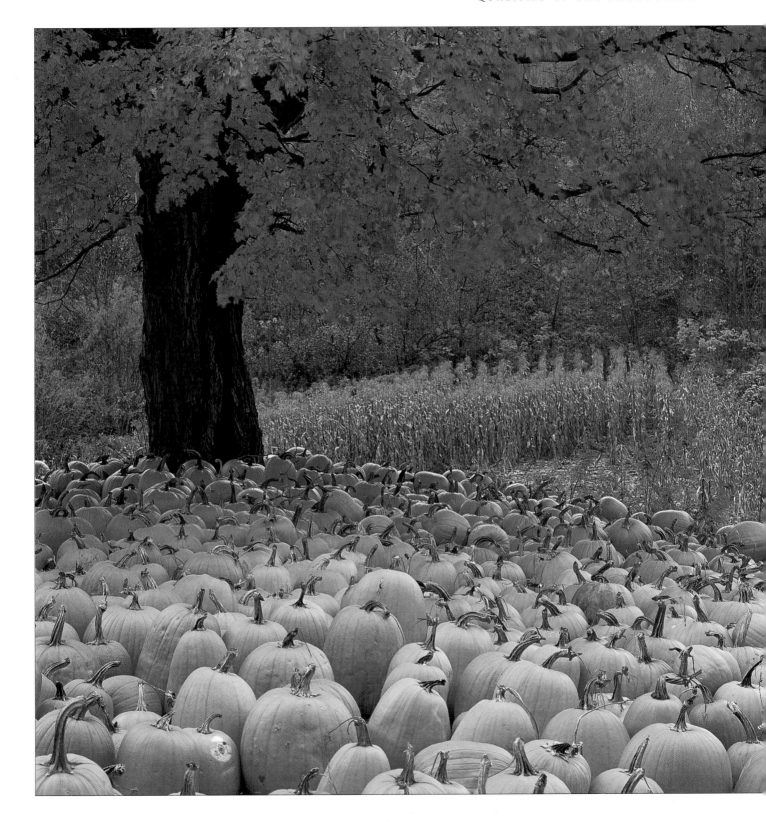

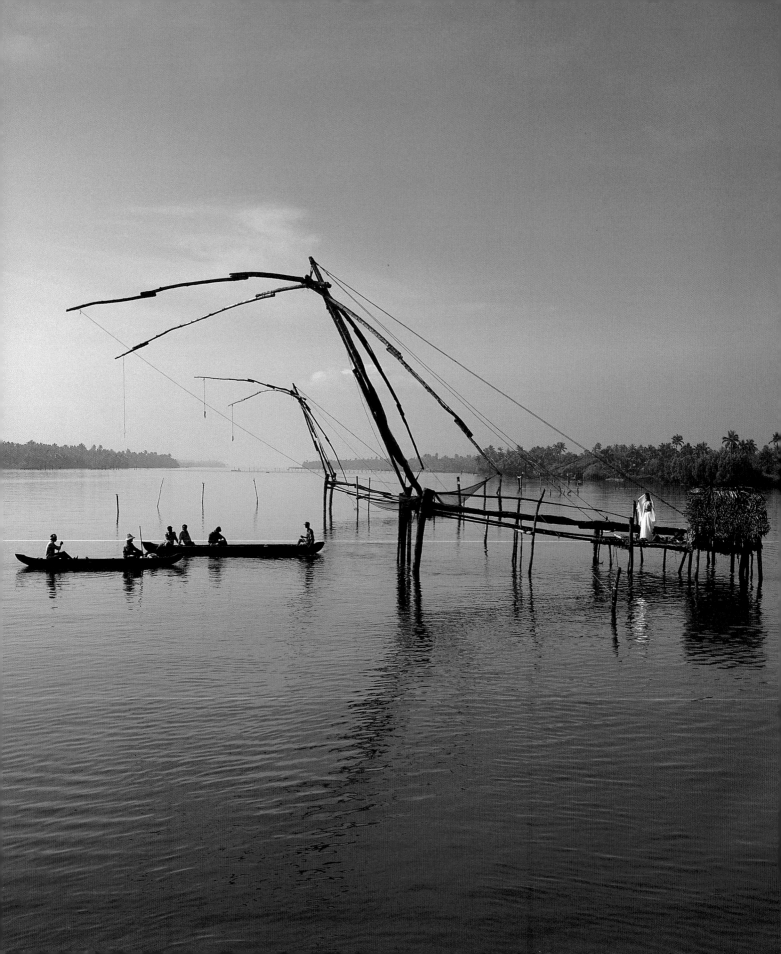

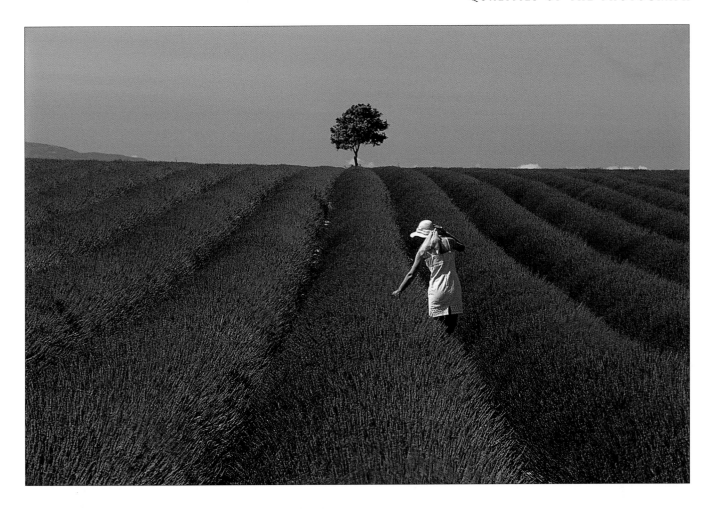

SETTING THE SCENE

A spidery traditional fishing structure combines with the boats to make a pleasing pattern against the predominantly cool background. The figure on the deck introduces a splash of white and yellow, which draws the eye into the composition. This is a piece of theater – this graceful figure is out of context and I particularly like the way the figures in the boats have become an audience. The absence of figures in my landscapes has been commented on, so this is a bit of a departure. I like the viewer to feel that he or she is the first visitor in an otherwise empty landscape.

Location: KERALA, INDIA

Camera: 6cm x 6cm; Lens: 50mm; Film: Fuji 100 ASA
Exposure: ⅟₁₅ second at f.16–22; Filter: polarizer

BALANCING THE PHOTOGRAPH

Again a single figure was deliberately introduced. It took about half an hour to find the right location. Interestingly, the location that worked best was on the intersection of the one-third division of the horizontal and vertical axes – a point that has traditionally been found to have the most visual impact. The banks of lavender converge and lead the eye to the tree on the horizon, and flow on and over the horizon so you don't know where they finish. But this picture is really about vast swathes of gorgeous color!

Location: PROVENCE, FRANCE

Camera: 35mm; Lens: 28mm; Film: Fuji 100 ASA;
Exposure: ⅛ second at f.22; Filter: polarizer

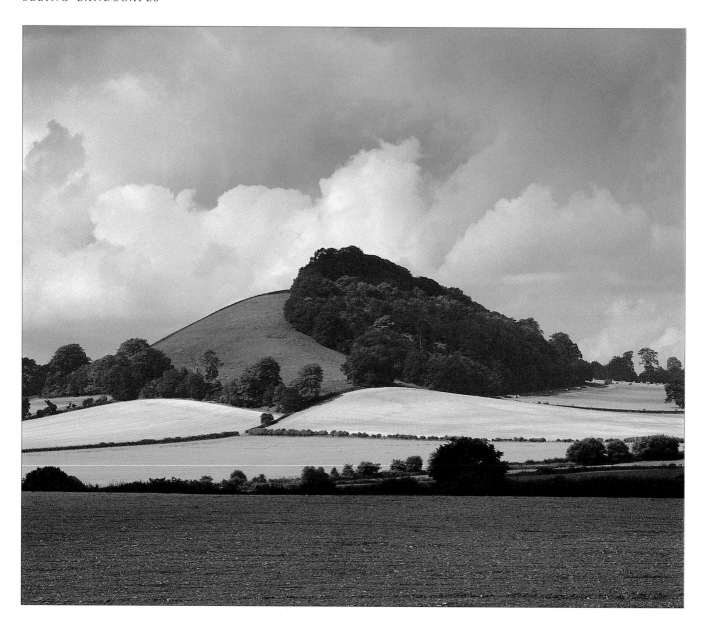

CHALK DOWNLAND WITHOUT CLOUD SHADOW

I am fond of this picture because it is not obviously photogenic. I like the interlocking geometry of the fields and the hill, and the contrast of the hedges and patches of woodland. However, in this version the picture falls away slightly at the top – the edge of the hill is not as crisply defined as I would wish. Note the differences between film stock.

Location: WILTSHIRE, ENGLAND

Camera: 6cm x 6cm; Lens: 250mm; Film: Fuji 50 ASA; Exposure: 1 second at f.45

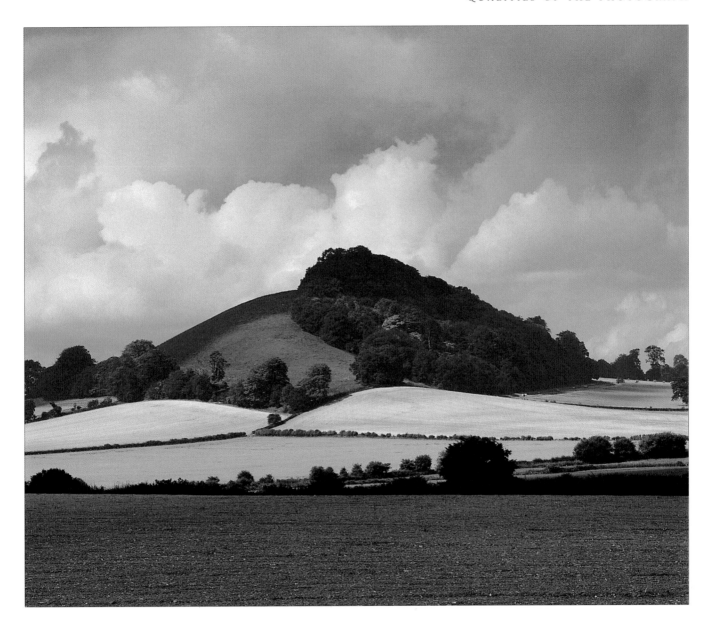

CHALK DOWNLAND WITH CLOUD SHADOW

I lingered at this location for some time, waiting for the light and the cloud to light my set as I wished. And look at the difference a tiny bit of light makes – with shadow delineating the top of the hill, it matches up with the hedgerows to complete the image. It becomes a series of triangles with sharp defining lines.

Location: Wiltshire, England

Camera: 6cm x 6cm; Lens: 250mm; Film: Agfa 50 ASA; Exposure: 1 second at f.45

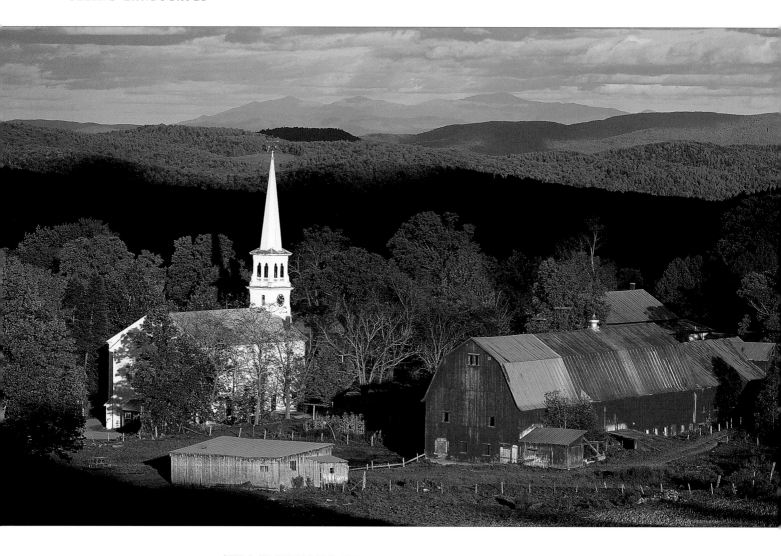

SIX MINUTES TO THREE

This pair of pictures illustrates how the mood and appearance of the landscape are transformed by light. Light can be used to conceal as well as to reveal, and if you are fortunate and patient, you can use cloud to design the lighting of your 'set'. So look up at the sky. Hopefully a cloud will deliver a shadow to a particular place. In this version an ugly building in the foreground is clearly visible.

Location: VERMONT, USA

Camera: 6cm x 17cm, cropped image; Lens: 300mm;
Film: Fuji 50 ASA; Exposure: 1 second at f.45

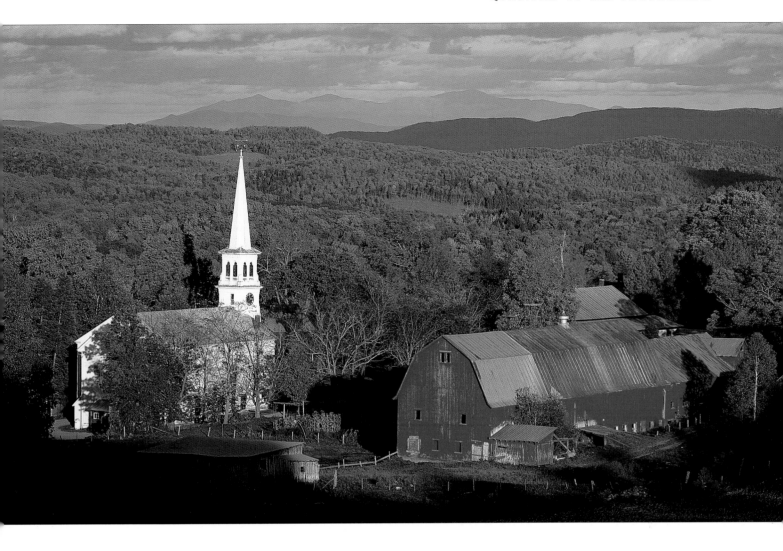

TWO MINUTES TO THREE

At six minutes to three there was no land shadow, but four minutes later the sun going down sent the shadow 20ft (6m) higher – nearly to the top of the tree. Notice how dense this shadow is and how it hides the offending building.

Location: VERMONT, USA

Camera: 6cm x 17cm, cropped image; Lens: 300mm;
Film: Fuji 50 ASA; Exposure: 1 second at f.45

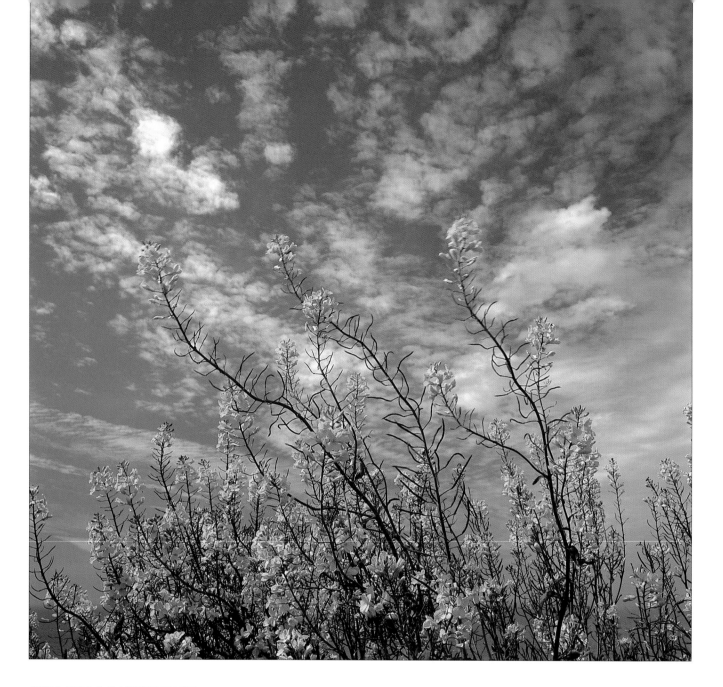

YELLOW AGAINST BLUE

Toward the end of the afternoon, the clouds that had peppered the sky all day spread out in fingers – a wonderful potential backdrop. I searched along the clifftop for a suitable subject to place in front of the sky, and I was delighted to find this profusion of flowers leaning in the same direction as the clouds. It seems that all the components are stretching together toward an unseen source or to revel in the bright sunshine.

Location: Cornwall, England

Camera: 6cm x 6cm; Lens: 50mm; Film: Fuji 50 ASA;
Exposure: ⅟₁₅ second at f.11–16; Filter: polarizer

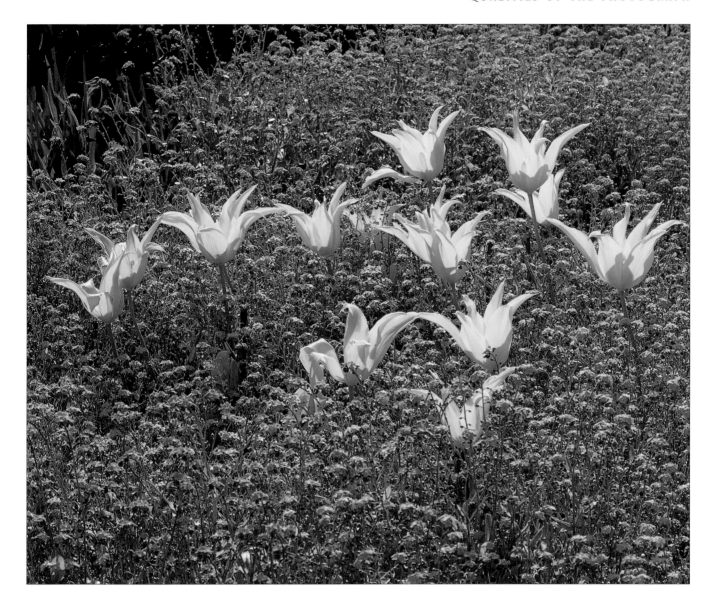

YELLOW AMID BLUE

Flowers provide swatches of gorgeous color, but for me the secret of successful flower
photographs is abundance and exuberance. The exploding starbust shapes of the yellow
tulips sizzle against the blue background, and I love the light and shade within the
flowers. To my mind the picture falls away at the top left, but I couldn't crop this
area out of the frame without stepping on all the lovely blue flowers.

Location: SUSSEX, ENGLAND

Camera: 6cm x 6cm; Lens: 150mm; Film: Fuji 50 ASA; Exposure: ¼ second at f.22–32

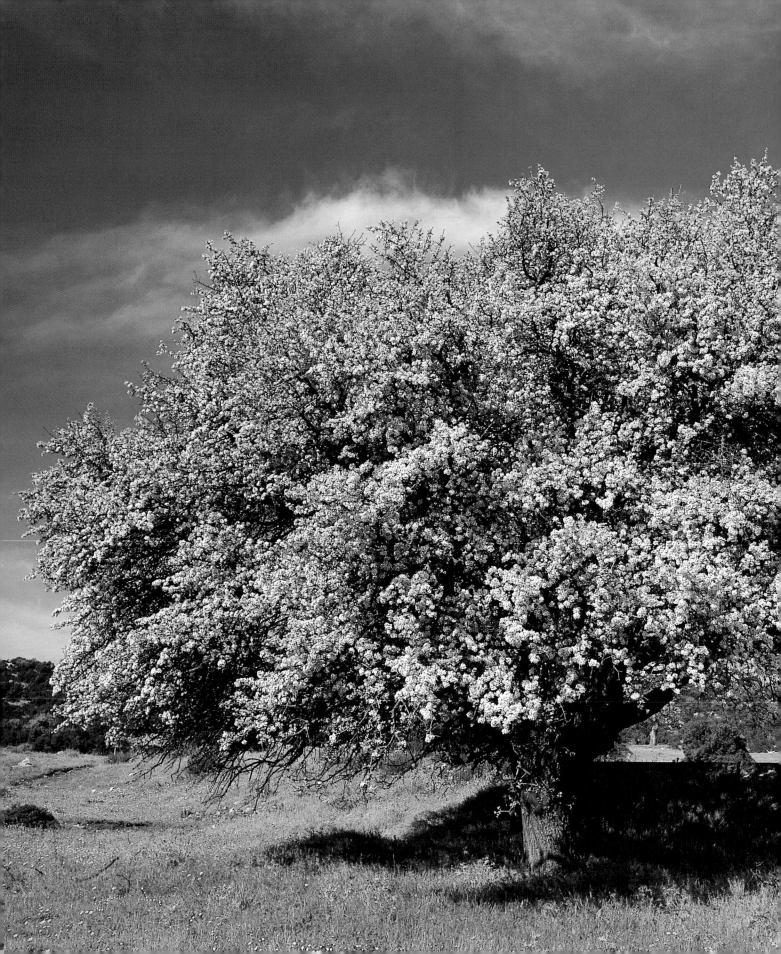

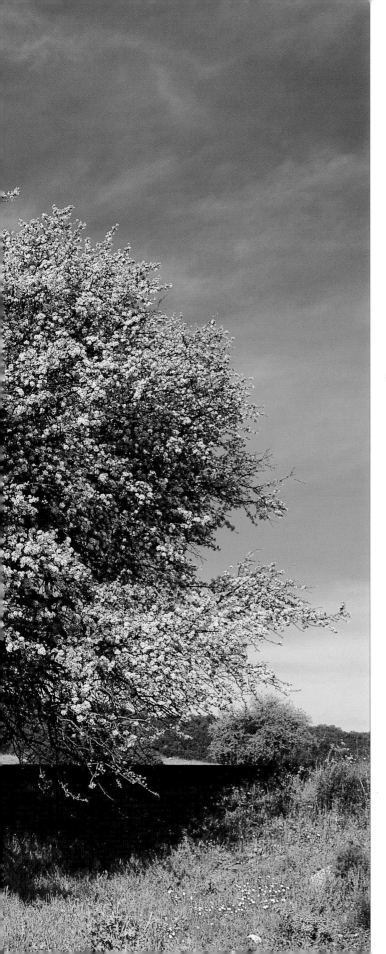

Elements of the Landscape

The underlying geology and millennia of evolution have created the contours of the landscape. Vegetation shrouds and softens outlines, while light, weather, time of day, and the seasons transform its appearance. The sky is the source of light and is the backcloth to the scenes enacted below. These natural components of the landscape are a rich and inexhaustible source of subjects and themes for the landscape photographer.

THE THORN TREE

The branches of this chunky tree were laden with creamy white blossom, tinged with apple green, and it seemed so happy with itself that I had to take its picture. I cropped in tightly to exclude extraneous matter – but there is still some confusion to the left. The flowers pick up the color and texture of the blossom. In an ideal world, the sky would have come right down behind the tree, making a perfect silhouette.

Location: THE LOT, FRANCE

Camera: 6cm x 6cm; Lens: 150mm;
Film: Fuji 50 ASA; Exposure: $\frac{1}{15}$ second at f.16

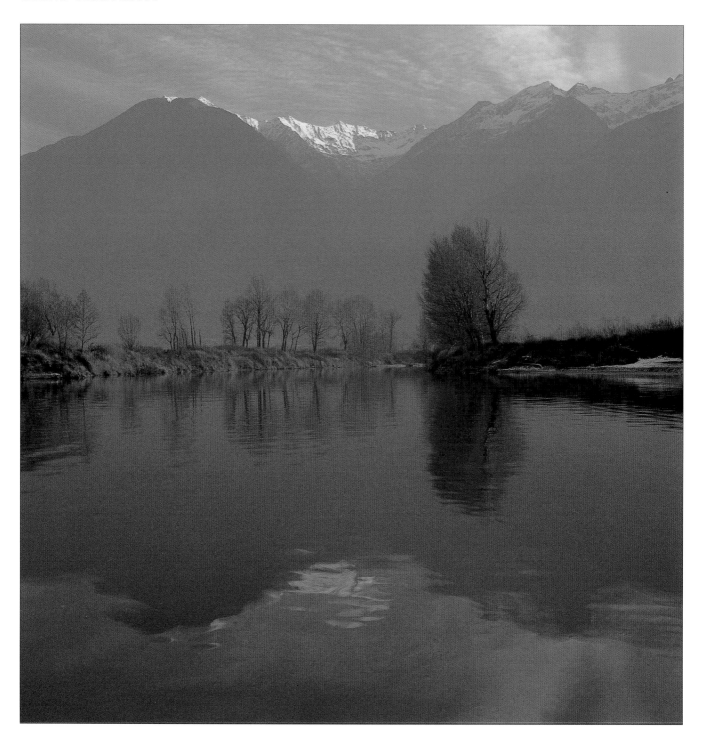

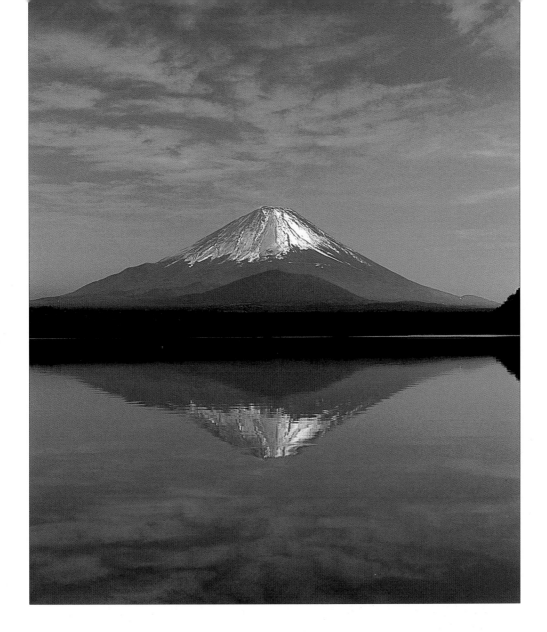

REFLECTED DRAMA

This mountainous landscape and its reflection make a single satisfying shape, creating a symmetry about the axis of the lake's edge. The tawny colors of February are set off by the bright sky and the dazzling white of the snowy peaks. The tree on the edge of the lake falls on the one-third division of the frame, a split that is almost universally found to be pleasing. Its reflection doubles its height and increases the impact of its vertical thrust.

Location: LOMBARDY, ITALY

Camera: 6cm x 6cm; Lens: 80mm;
Film: Fuji 50 ASA; Exposure: ⅛ second at f.16

SNOW-CAPPED SYMMETRY

This must surely be one of the most photographed, and instantly recognizable, mountains in the world. The cone of the volcano has a symmetry that is rarely seen in nature and its reflection in the glassy surface of the lake creates another symmetry. The clouds that appear to fan out from the mountain peak are crucial to the success of the image – 10 minutes later they had dispersed.

Location: MOUNT FUJI, JAPAN

Camera: 6cm x 6cm; Lens: 50mm; Film: Fuji 50 ASA;
Exposure: ¼ second at f.22; Filter: polarizer, 50%

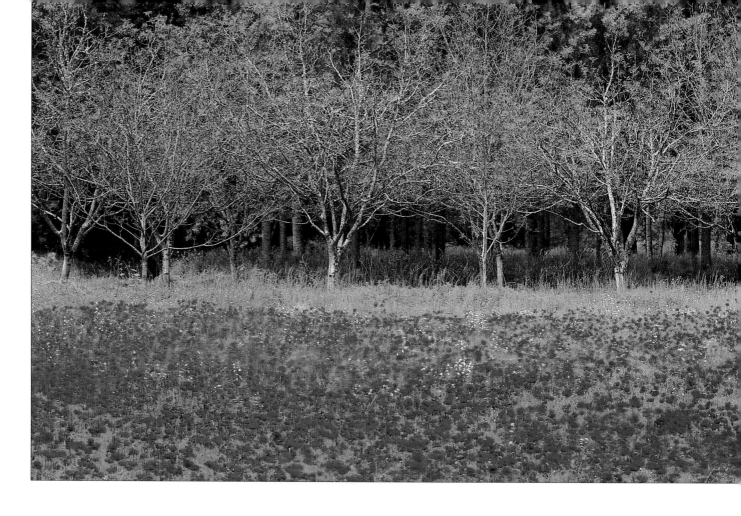

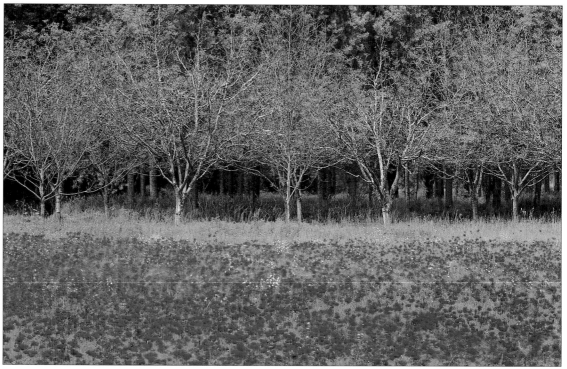

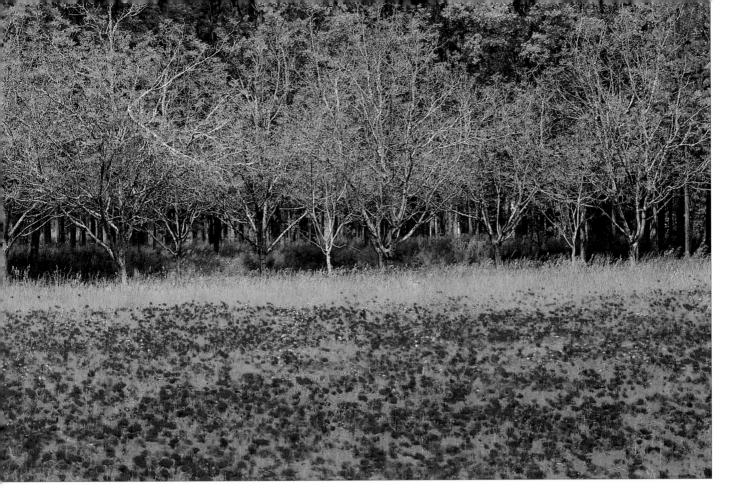

LAYERED LANDSCAPE

I glimpsed this lovely tree-lined avenue from the road as I was driving by. Such
fleeting images are complete and perfect in the mind's eye, but trying to recreate them
in the camera is not easy. I spent 45 minutes finding the track and the viewpoint from
which I could try to reconstruct my vision. At first glance, the trees seem regularly spaced
and the path looks straight, but on closer inspection the image is less 'perfect' towards the
right-hand side. The path rises so that the band of green grass gets wider, and there are
distracting shafts of light coming through the trees. Other imperfections include a broken
branch and the boughs of dark, glossy-green foliage, which are entirely out of sympathy
with the rest of the image. In constructing my pictures I am trying to find order in, or
impose order on, the randomness of Nature. For all these reasons I find the smaller
version cropped from the left side of the panoramic photograph much more satisfying.

Location: THE LOT, FRANCE

Camera: 6cm x 17cm; Lens: 300mm;
Film: Fuji 50 ASA; Exposure: 2 seconds at f.64

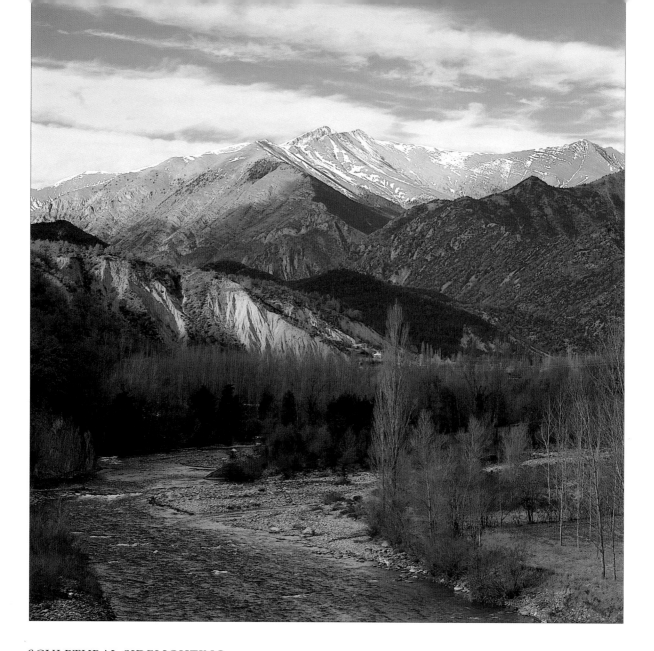

SCULPTURAL SIDELIGHTING

Sharp winter light slanting in from the side gives this sculpted landscape a strange and surreal feeling. I waited for the light and shadow to travel across the landscape so that certain parts were spotlit and others were hidden in shadow. A more overall light would have been less dramatic. The eye looks for the lightest highlight – here the contest is between the bright, white snow and the sunbathed cliffs in the middle distance. These illuminated rocks appear especially bright because they are surrounded by darkness.

Location: LÉRIDA, SPAIN

Camera: 6cm x 6cm; Lens: 150mm; Film: Fuji 50 ASA;
Exposure: ¹⁄₃₀ second at f.11; Filters: polarizer, 81B (warm up)

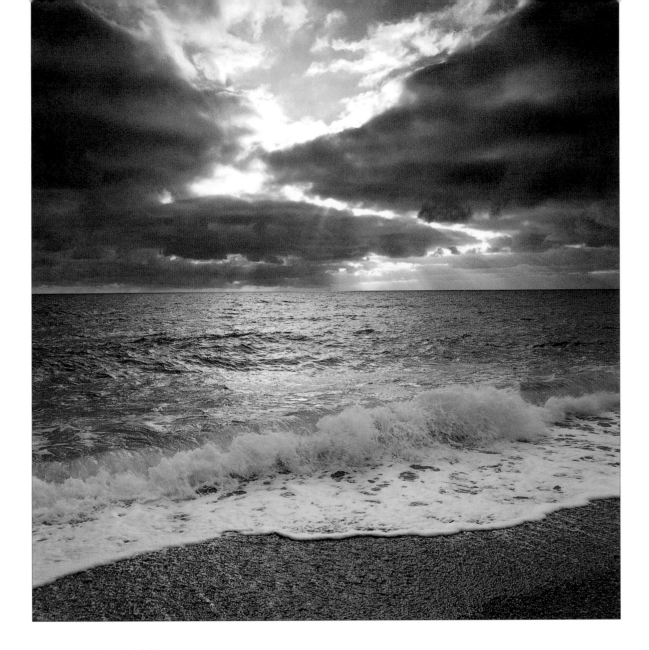

CREATING DRAMA

I confess – this picture is a lie! The cloud with its zig-zag fissures was there, but it wasn't as dark as it appears in the picture, and everything was much cooler and grayer. I used a graduated filter to darken the sky and introduce a sense of drama artificially. The filter also warms everything slightly and imposes a sense of unity. Filters should be used modestly, in fact it should not be apparent that you have used one. Remember that a filter can make a good photograph better, but it can't make a bad photograph good – use of a filter should never be conspicuous.

Location: DORSET, ENGLAND

Camera: 6cm x 6cm; Lens: 50mm; Film: Fuji 50 ASA; Exposure: $\frac{1}{15}$ second at f.11; Filters: medium-density, graduated, 81C (warm up)

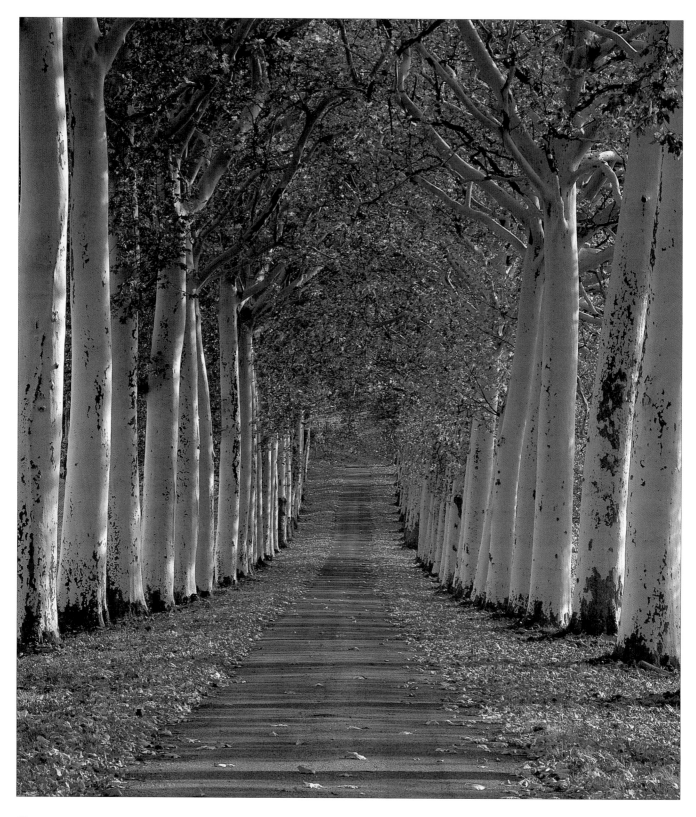

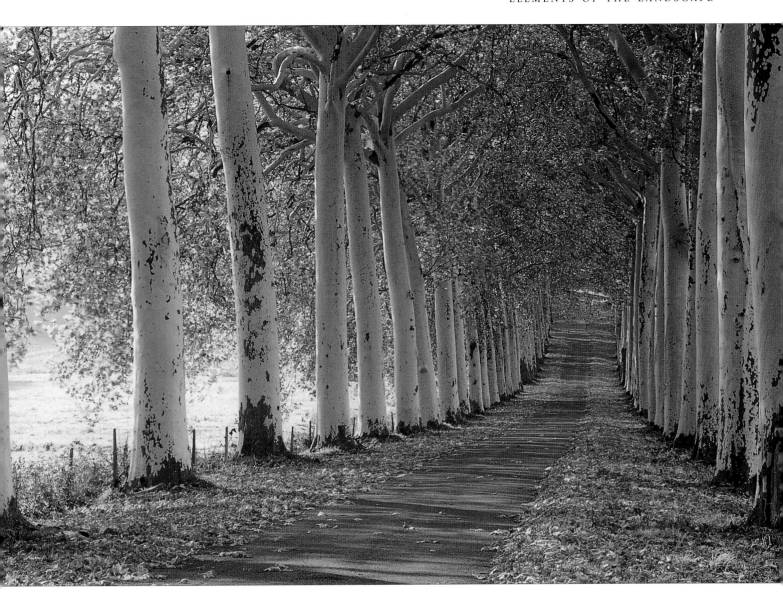

AVENUE OF GOLD: 1

Avenues of trees are a recurrent theme in photography – there is always a mystery about where they are going and what lies at the end. This colonnade has the symmetry of a cathedral, lit by the golden light that slants between the tree trunks and filters through the burnished foliage.

Location: NEAR ÉPERNAY, FRANCE

Camera: 6cm x 6cm; Lens: 150mm;
Film: Fuji 50 ASA; Exposure: ½ second at f.22–32

AVENUE OF GOLD: 2

This image has more direct light and is brighter, more colorful and less austere. I stood to one side so the avenue swept in at an angle, creating a sense of movement that draws you into and across the image. This gives a glimpse of the world beyond, and the fence provides a sense of scale.

Location: NEAR ÉPERNAY, FRANCE

Camera: 35mm; Lens: 130mm;
Film: Fuji 50 ASA; Exposure: ¼ second at f.22

WILDFLOWER WILDERNESS

This profusion of glorious color was quite heady. I wandered for half an hour looking for the ideal vantage point, and then waited a further 30 minutes for the total stillness necessary for a long exposure. I gave most weight to the poppies, but the yellow flowers suggest shafts of sunlight. I would have liked a little cloud to soften the sky, but by framing to give a high horizon I prevented the intense blue from dominating the photograph.

Location: ANDALUSIA, SPAIN

Camera: 6cm x 17cm; Lens: 105mm; Film: Fuji 50 ASA;
Exposure: 2 seconds at f.64; Filter: polarizer

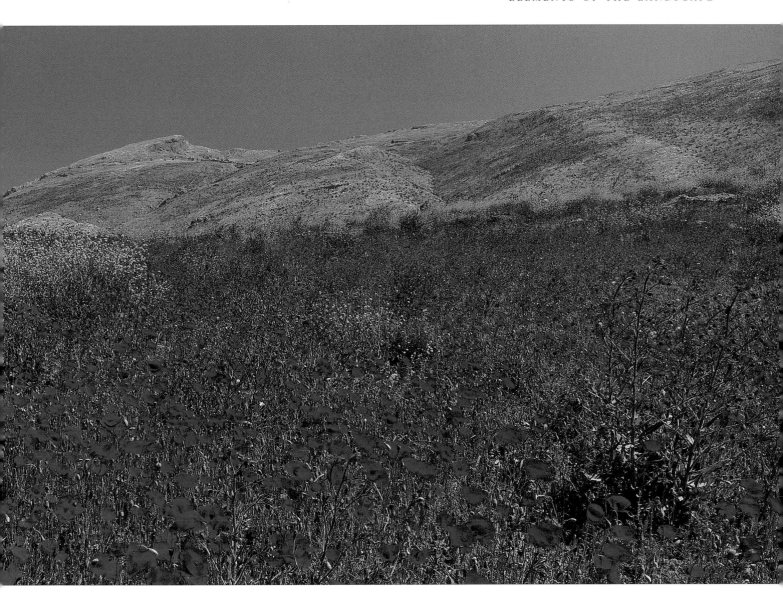

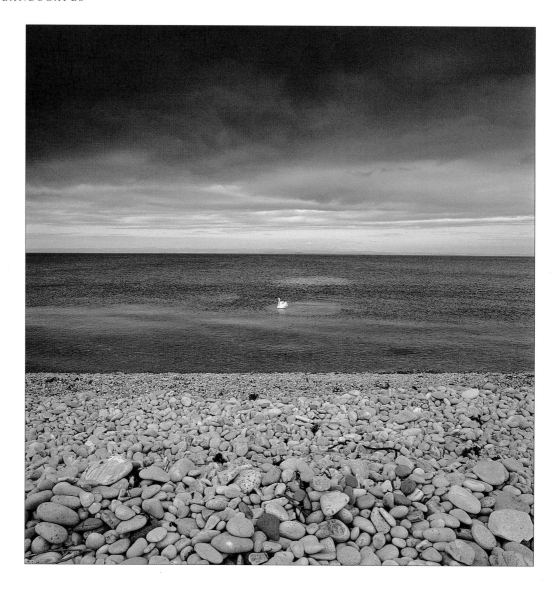

BANDS OF COLOR AND TEXTURE

The pebbles in the foreground are smooth, and in sharp focus, the sea has a crinkled metallic quality, while the sky is gray and foreboding, with a sliver of brightness on the horizon. When the swan appeared I thought I had lost my picture – but then I realized it actually made it.

Location: ISLAY, INNER HEBRIDES, SCOTLAND

Camera: 6cm x 6cm; Lens: 50mm;
Film: Fuji 100 ASA; Exposure: ⅟₃₀ second at f.11

STUDY IN BLUE

This image was compelling. The light was crisp and bright, a rainstorm had just passed overhead. I used a medium density filter as I wanted to emphasize the dark, threatening sky. The filter compresses the brightness range and is a nifty device.

Location: CORFU, GREECE

Camera: 6cm x 6cm; Lens: 50mm;
Film: Fuji 50 ASA; Exposure: ⅟₁₅ second at f.11;
Filters: medium-density, graduated

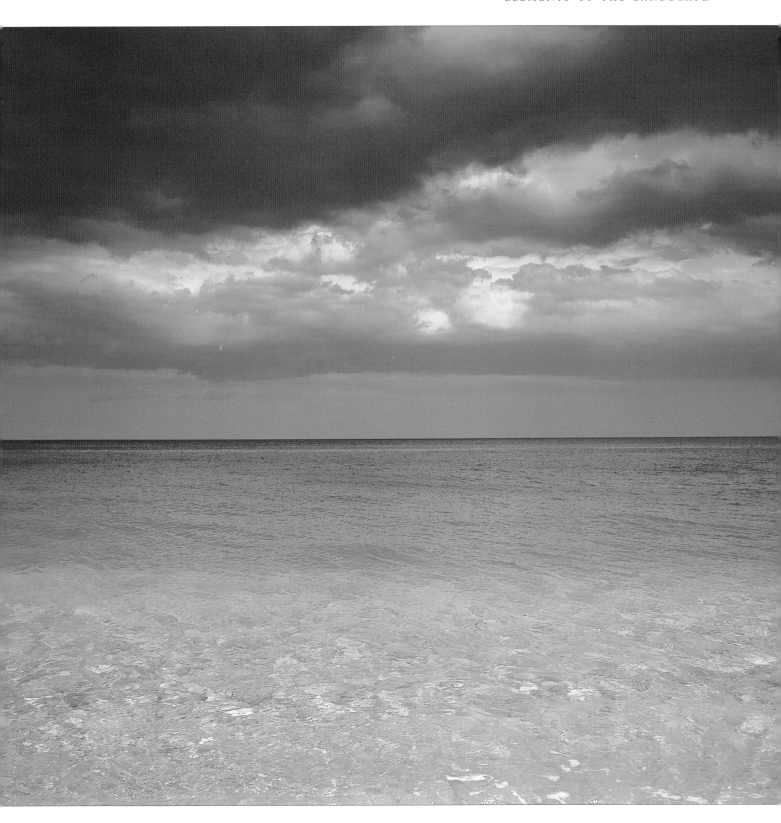

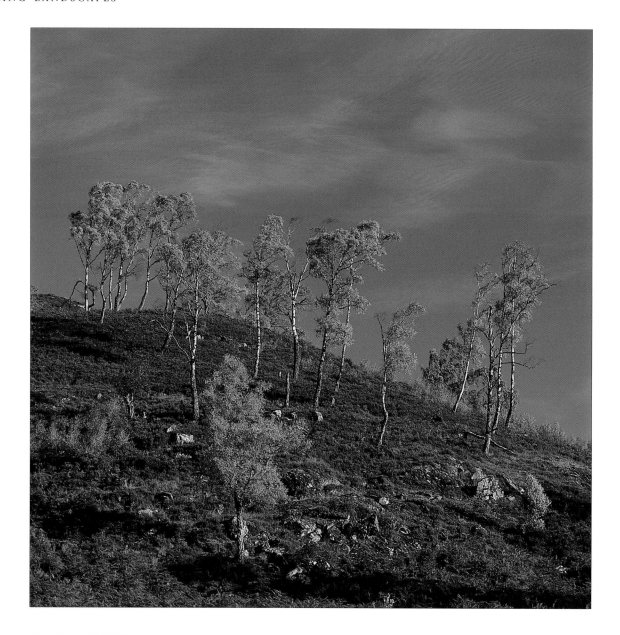

GOLD ON BLUE

This picture was rushed as the precious white cirrus was being whisked away.
The bright sidelight ripples across the silvery tree trunks. I would have liked
more sense of wind, but only one tree at the top left looks really windblown.
The gilded foliage works well against the blue sky.

Location: HIGHLAND, SCOTLAND

Camera: 6cm x 6cm; Lens: 150mm; Film: Fuji 50 ASA;
Exposure: ⅓₀ second at f.8–11; Filter: polarizer

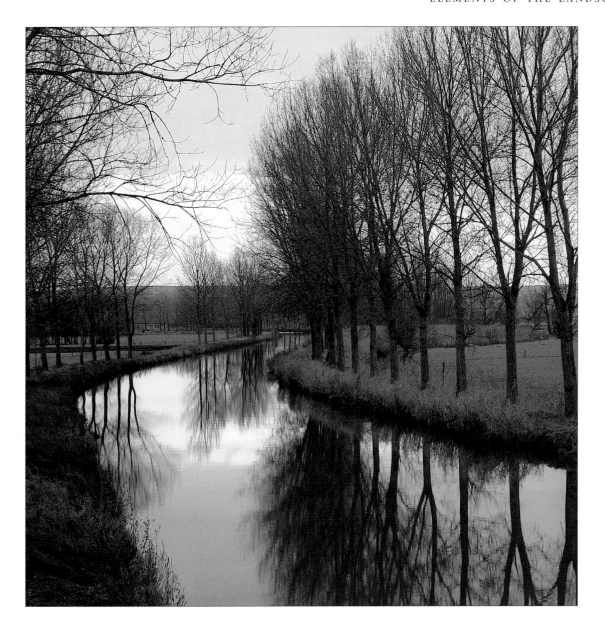

USING REFLECTION

Canals in France always have a line of trees marking their course. The sweep of the canal draws us in and the reflection of the trees in the surface of the water creates repetitions and symmetries. The muted fall colors and the velvety black trees look wonderful against the evening sky.

Location: ARDENNES, FRANCE

Camera: 6cm x 6cm; Lens: 150mm; Film: Fuji 50 ASA;
Exposure: 1/30 second at f.11; Filter: 81B (warm up)

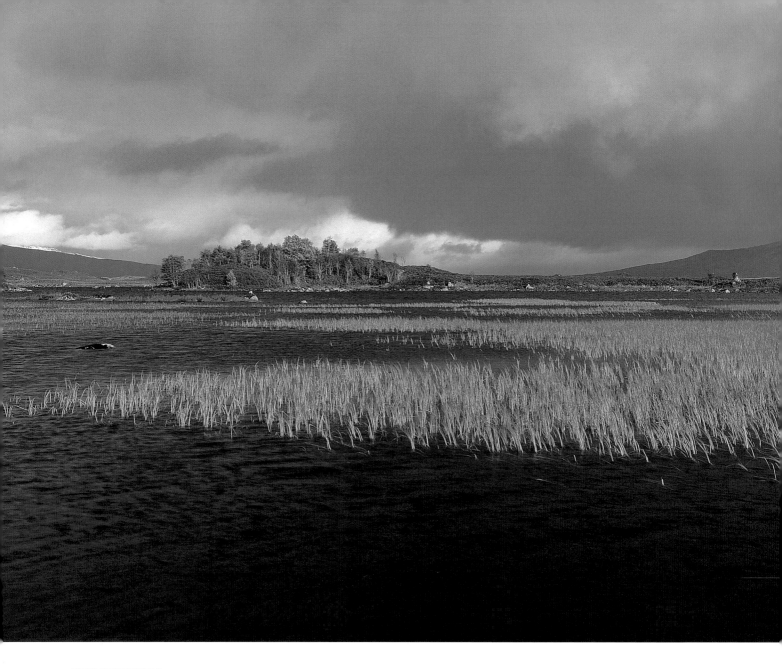

WILDERNESS

Rannoch Moor is one of the last unspoiled wildernesses in Britain and one of my favorite places. A bed of reeds emerges from the inky-black, peaty waters – soft and feathery in lovely yellows and oranges, they look out of place in this hostile environment. The surrounding landscape is suffused with glorious colors – old golds and coral pinks, russet and earth brown. The clouds form a vortex, which appears to emerge from the distant peak.

Location: RANNOCH MOOR, SCOTLAND

Camera: 6cm x 17cm; Lens: 105mm; Film: Fuji 100 ASA;
Exposure: ⅛ second at f.22; Filter: polarizer, 50%

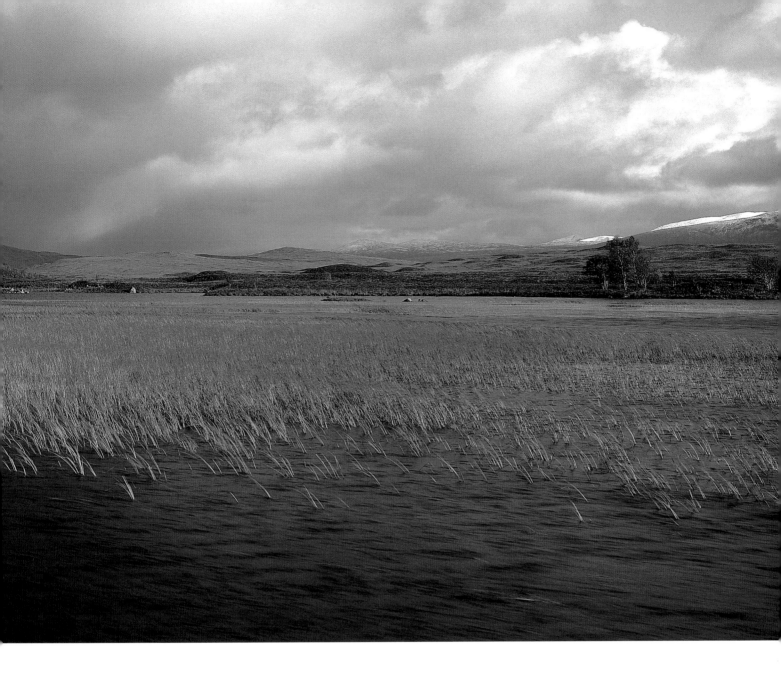

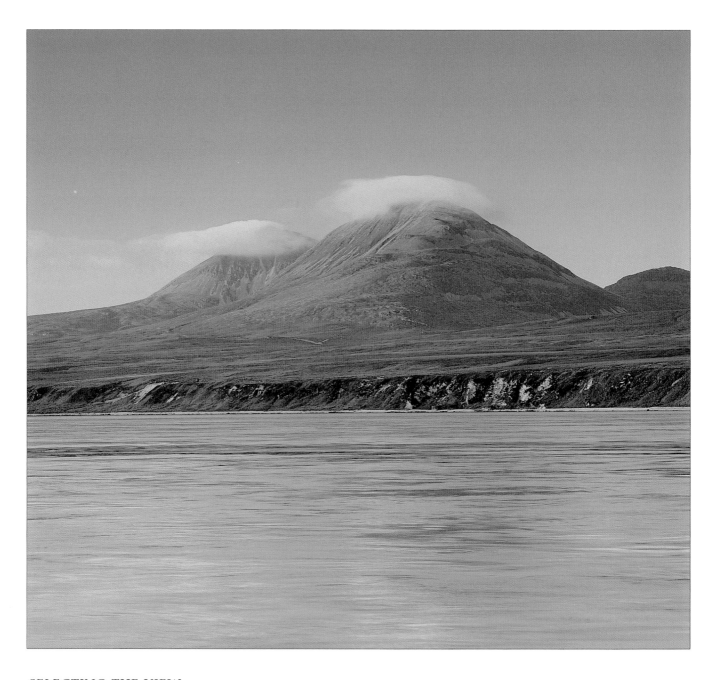

SELECTING THE VIEW

The breeze ruffles the surface of the moving water, creating horizontal striations that echo those on the land and disrupt the reflections of the mountains. The diffuse evening light drenches the scene in a soft, pink glow, including the puffs of cloud on the twin peaks. By carefully choosing my viewpoint, I positioned the mountains on a horizontal raft of land.

Location: JURA, INNER HEBRIDES, SCOTLAND

Camera: 6cm x 6cm; Lens: 50mm; Film: Kodak 64 ASA;
Exposure: ⅛ second at f.22; Filter: polarizer

70

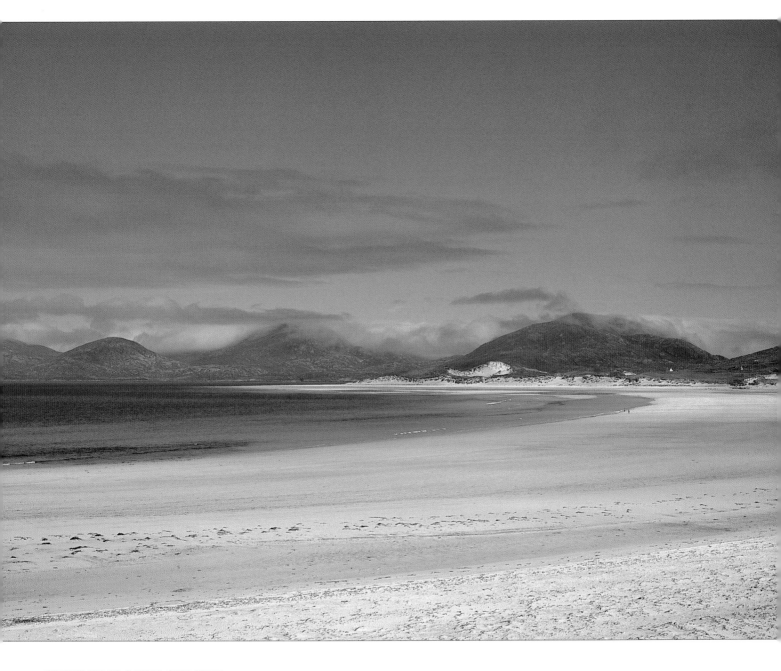

VIEW FROM THE STRAND

This photograph encompasses many disparate features – white sand, blue-green sea, and a chain of barren gray mountains. The pictures that work for me are those in which there is a sense of order and deliberation. Here I have placed the chain of mountains right at the center of the picture, and ensured that the disk of cloud occupies and mirrors the sea.

Location: HARRIS, SCOTLAND

Camera: 6cm x 6cm; Lens: 50mm; Film: Fuji 50 ASA;
Exposure: ⅟₆₀ second at f.8–11; Filter: polarizer

71

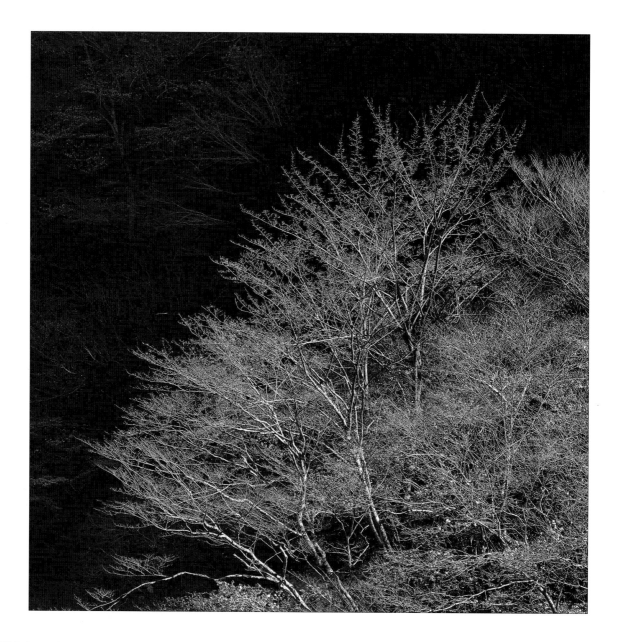

SILVER FILIGREE

This combination of strong, raking light against deep shadow occurs only in mountainous regions and rarely in summer. Every branch and twig is brilliantly lit on one side, with the opposite side in shadow, so that all the details are depicted with precision. I like the upswept branches and the way light and dark occupy equal areas.

Location: HONSHU, JAPAN

Camera: 6cm x 6cm; Lens: 150mm;
Film: Fuji 50 ASA; Exposure: ⅟₁₅ second at f.16

RED AND RUSSET

The russet maple foliage is stunningly lit by the sun, while the inky-black silhouettes of the trunk and branches have an emphatic quality. There are several elements that cannot be excluded without slicing through branches, so although the photograph records the beauty of Nature, it is not a successful picture by my standards.

Location: HONSHU, JAPAN

Camera: 6cm x 6cm; Lens: 150mm;
Film: Fuji 100 ASA; Exposure: ⅟₁₅ second at f.22

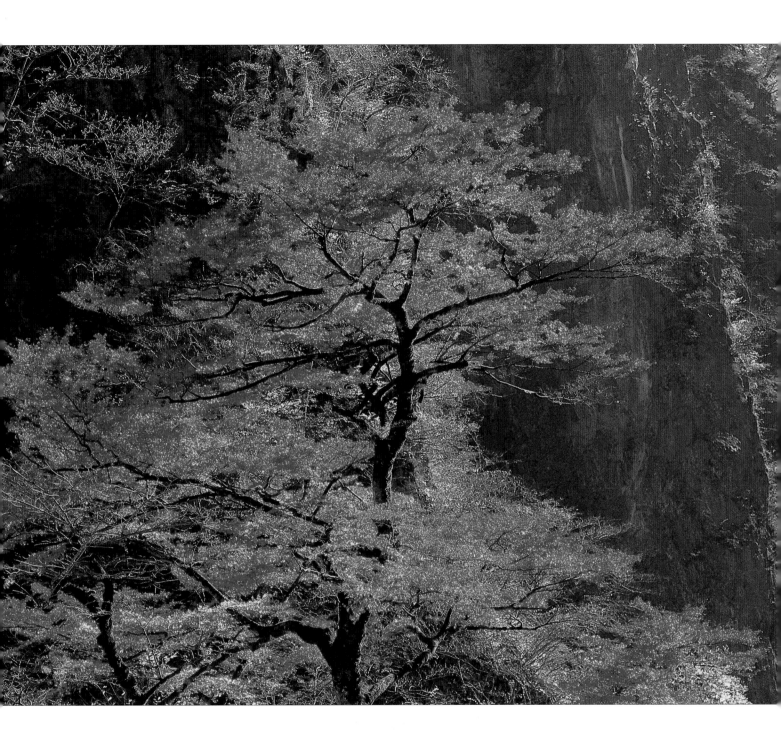

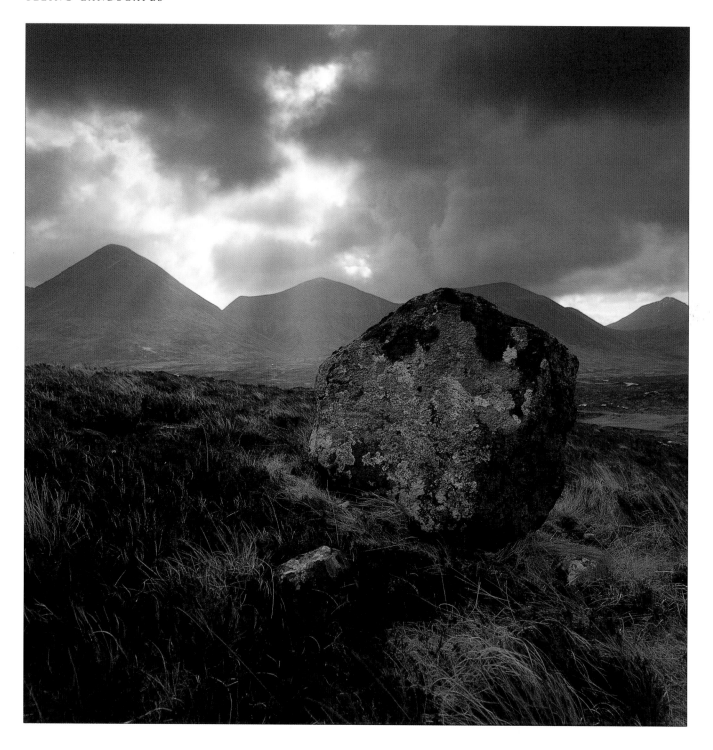

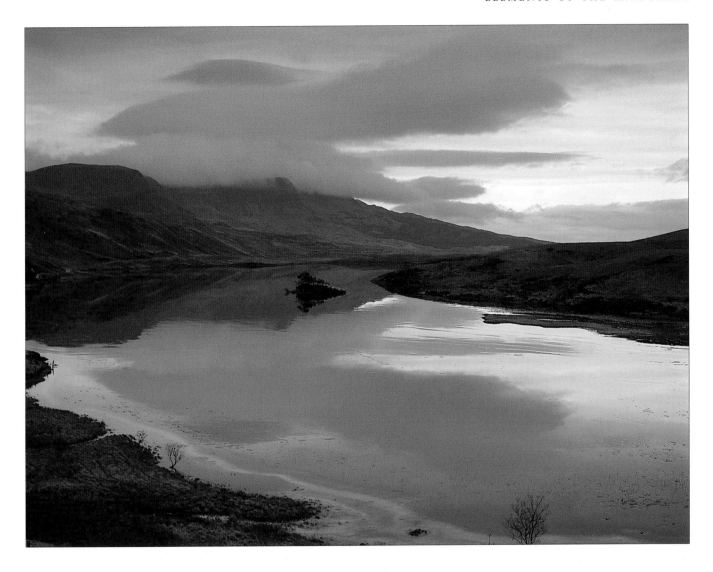

SHAPE AND COLOR

This lichen-covered boulder echoes the shapes of the hills beyond. I climbed a ladder to make it tuck neatly under the horizon and mirror the slope of the hill on the right and the harmonious grays and peaty browns of sky, landscape, and rock are pleasing. I used a graduated filter to add a sense of drama to the sky.

Location: ISLE OF SKYE, SCOTLAND

Camera: 6cm x 6cm; Lens: 50mm; Film: Fuji 100 ASA; Exposure: ⅛ second at f.22; Filters: low-density, graduated

AT THE MERCY OF THE ELEMENTS

This brooding picture was taken on a winter's day. The sky was dark and foreboding, and the water had the look of molten metal. I had to get 7ft (2.1m) above the ground to frame the picture the way I wanted – a different lens would have brought everything forward. The reflection of the sky creates a satisfying top-to-bottom symmetry.

Location: ISLE OF SKYE, SCOTLAND

Camera: 6cm x 6cm; Lens: 50mm; Film: Fuji 50 ASA; Exposure: $^1/_{15}$ second at f.8

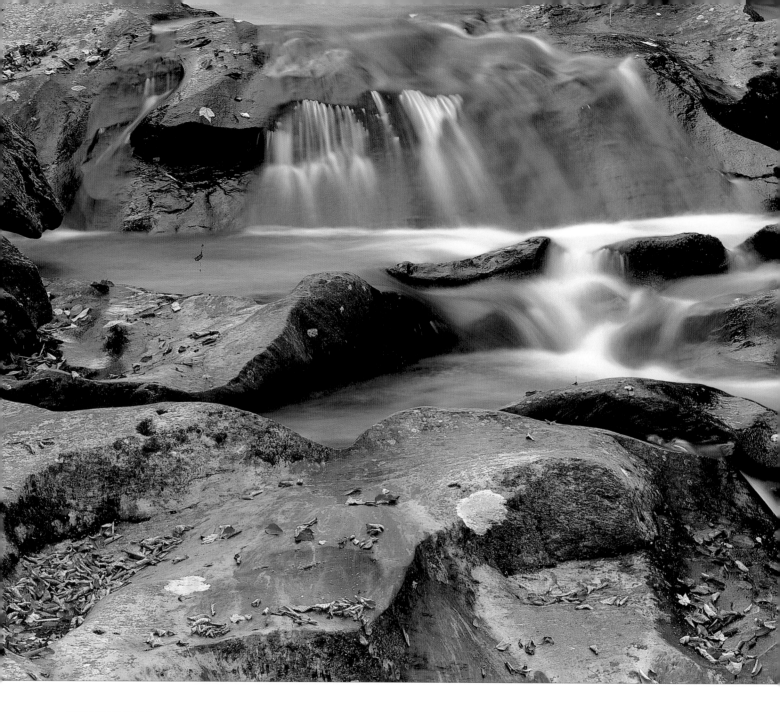

WATERFALLS

The combination of rocks, boulders, and tumbling water is an obvious subject, but if the shutter speed is not right the water will look solid. The correct shutter speed depends on the velocity of the water, so be prepared to experiment, and to use a lot of film. If possible, exclude the most turbulent water. Showing the source of the water helps to make sense of the landscape.

Location: VERMONT, USA

Camera: 6cm x 17cm, cropped image; Lens: 300mm;
Film: Fuji 50 ASA; Exposure: ⅛ second at f.64; Filter: polarizer

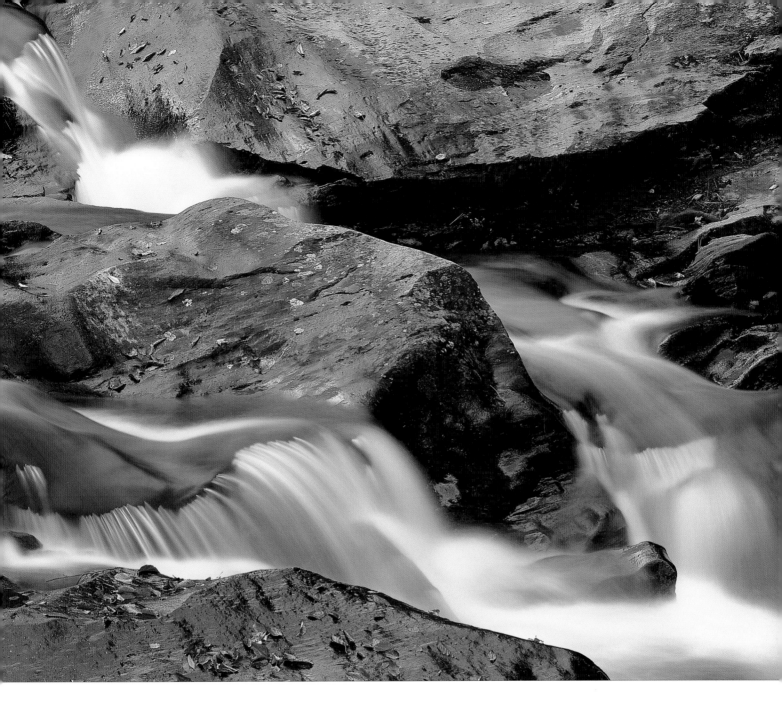

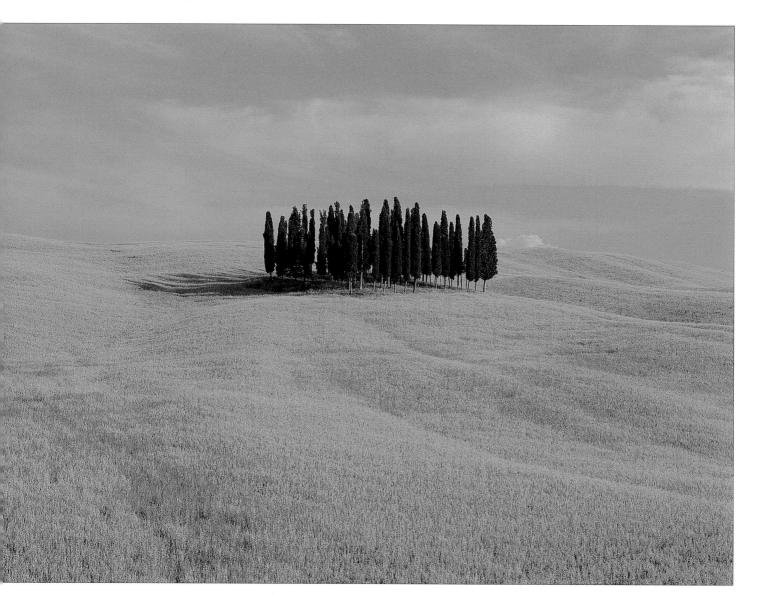

CYPRESS TREES, SPRING

Trees are most magnificent when isolated within the landscape. This regiment of trees, with its orderly formation, clean outline, and lance-like profiles, has an eerie quality. In this version, taken on a spring afternoon, the trees are set within a green fodder crop and a cloud-veiled sky.

Location: TUSCANY, ITALY

Camera: 6cm x 6cm; Lens: 150mm; Film: Fuji 50 ASA; Exposure: ⅟₃₀ second at f.11; Filter: polarizer

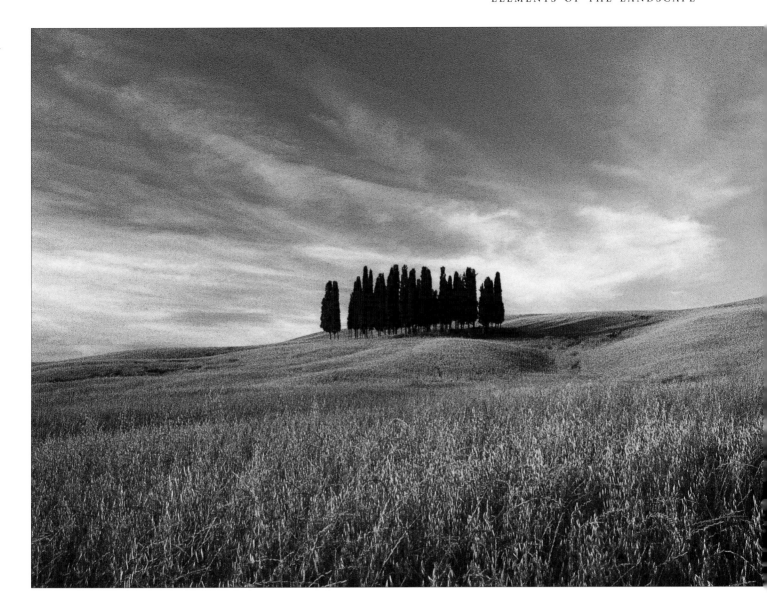

CYPRESS TREES, SUMMER

For this version, taken on a different occasion, I used a fast film
to give the image a grainy quality. This, together with the lower
viewpoint, swirling sky, and textured foreground, creates a sense
of depth and drama, which contrasts with the flatter, more
graphic quality of the version opposite.

Location: TUSCANY, ITALY

Camera: 35mm; Lens: 28mm; Film: Agfa 1000 ASA;
Exposure: 1/60 second at f.22; Filter: polarizer

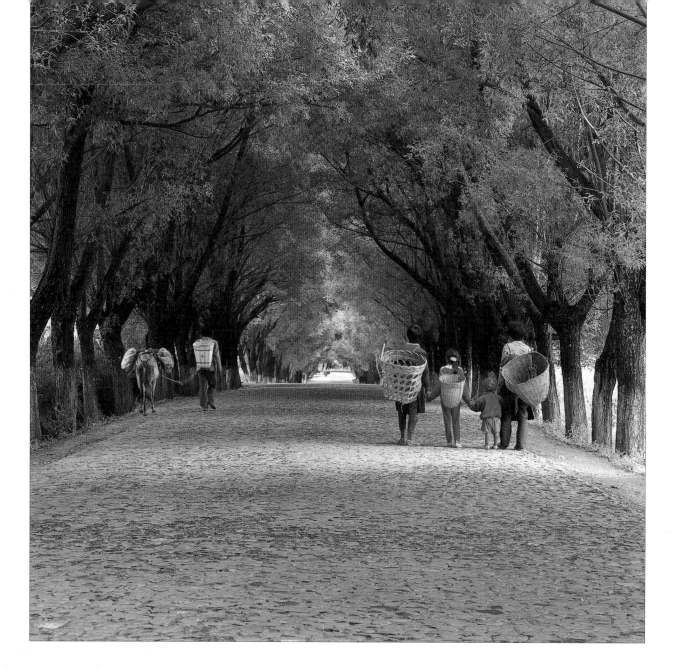

TREE TUNNEL: 1

The spreading branches of these dark, dense trees arch over the road to create a tunnel. The brightness in the distance, and the figures walking in that direction, draw you in. The red and pink garments enliven the scene, while the light in the foreground falls neatly beneath the group.

Location: LIJIANG, CHINA

Camera: 6cm x 6cm; Lens: 50mm;
Film: Fuji 100 ASA; Exposure: 1/30 second at f.11

TREE TUNNEL: 2

Tall poplars create a vertical architecture, so it is important to get up high to counteract the tendency for perspective to make verticals converge. The character of the foliage affects the quality of the light – poplars have small, fluttery leaves that create a flickering, dappled effect.

Location: VALENCIA, SPAIN

Camera: 6cm x 6cm; Lens: 50mm;
Film: Kodak 64 ASA; Exposure: 1/4 second at f.22

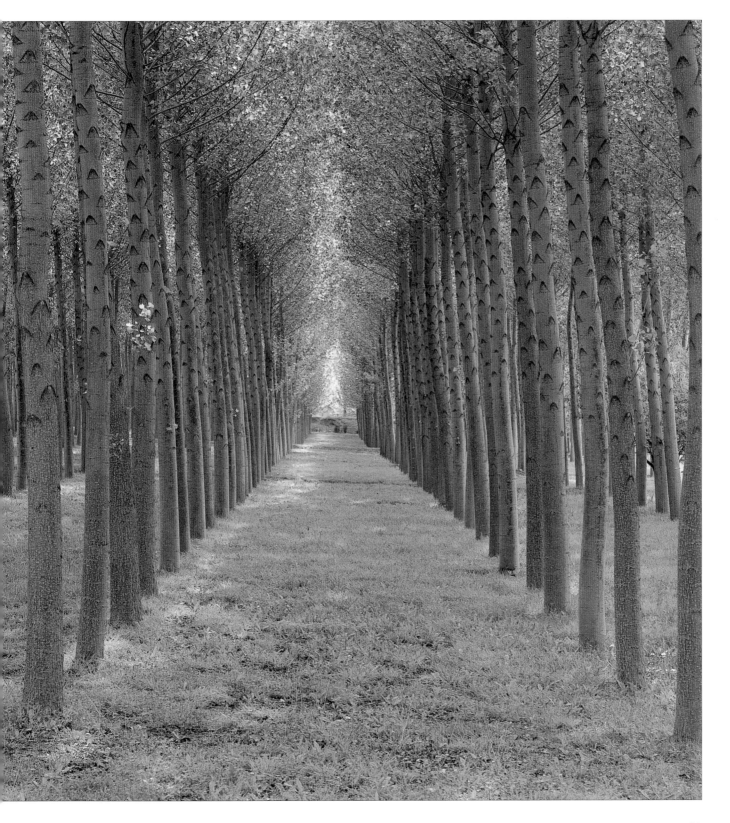

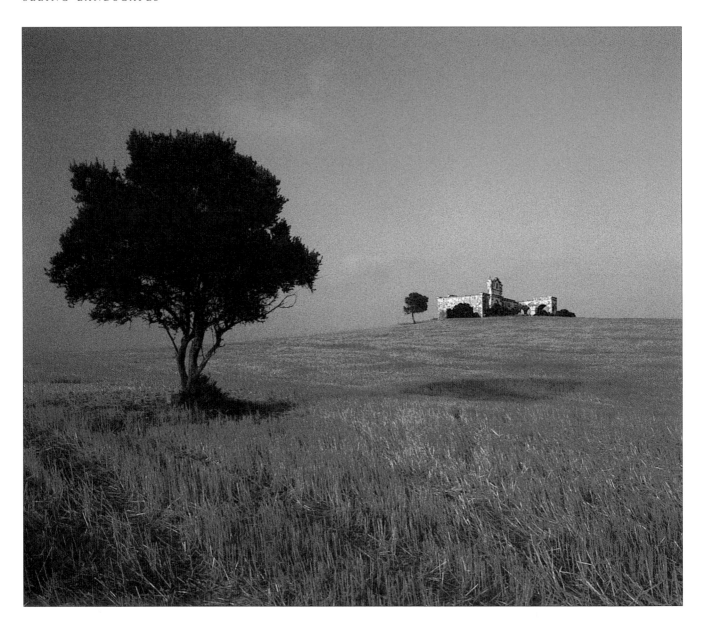

BALANCING WITH SHADOWS

The views from below this castle did not reveal its setting, and I like, where possible, to place my subjects on their own platforms. The stubble creates a recession to the castle on the hill, while the tree and its shadow frame the castle and close the picture. The shadow drops below the castle and occupies the same area. The horizon bisecting the tree is not ideal, but it is acceptable as it occurs near the tree's base. The 1000 ASA film produces a painterly effect.

Location: ANDALUSIA, SPAIN

Camera: 6cm x 6cm; Lens: 50mm; Film: Agfa 1000 ASA; Exposure: ¹⁄₆₀ second at f.22

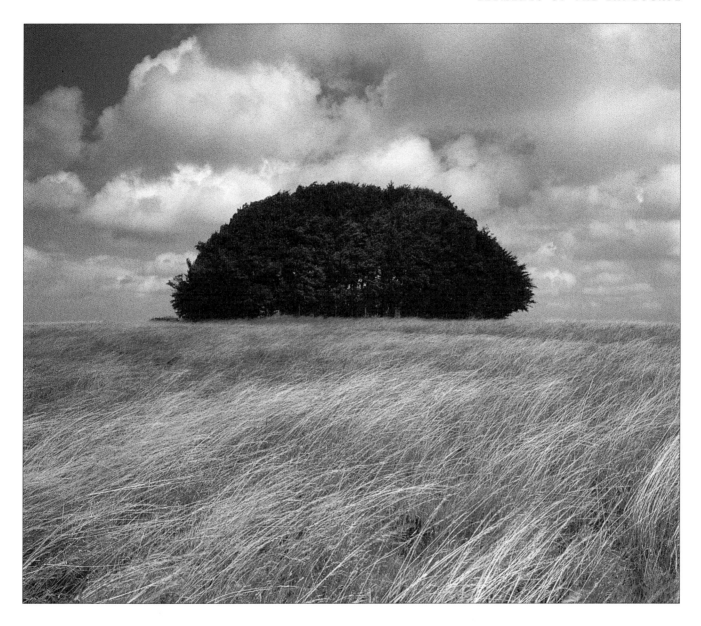

ABSTRACT BEECHES

The trees appear to have snuggled down just beyond the crest of the hill. As we cannot see their trunks clearly, an element of ambiguity is introduced, so that they become an abstract form within the deliberately simplified landscape. The bubbling clouds and the bending grasses suggest the weather, while the grainy film softens the colors and textures.

Location: WILTSHIRE, ENGLAND

Camera: 6cm x 6cm; Lens: 80mm; Film: Agfa 1000 ASA; Exposure: $\frac{1}{125}$ second at f.22

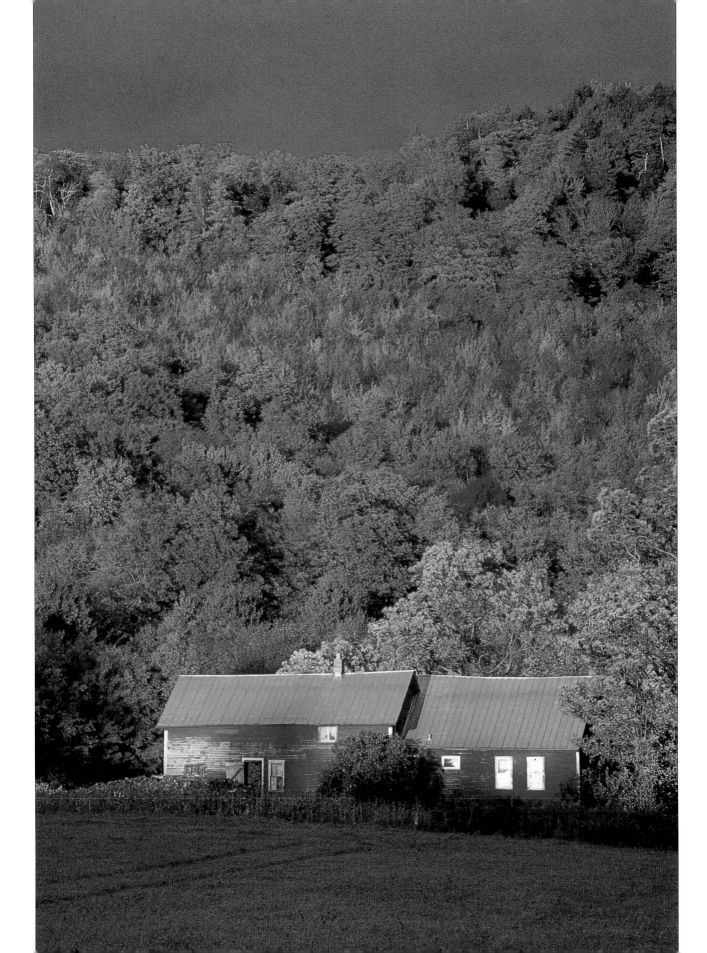

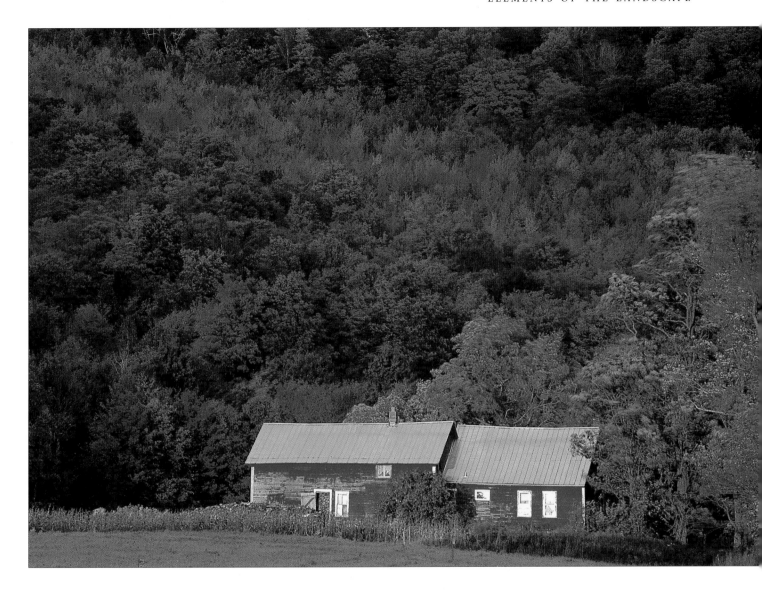

SUNLIT FOLIAGE

It was fall and the red paint of the barn and the foliage behind were lit by the setting sun. The show was over in five minutes, so these pictures were captured rather than made. Here I've used a portrait format and included dark sky and foreground, which emphasize the brilliant foliage.

Location: VERMONT, USA

Camera: 35mm; Lens: 280mm;
Film: Fuji 100 ASA; Exposure: $\frac{1}{15}$ second at f.16

SUNLIT BARN

In this version I've used a landscape format, eliminated the sky, and dropped the barn to the very bottom of the frame. The barn is spotlit in this last spasm of excitement before the light disappears.

Location: VERMONT, USA

Camera: 35mm; Lens: 230mm;
Film: Fuji 100 ASA; Exposure: $\frac{1}{15}$ second at f.16

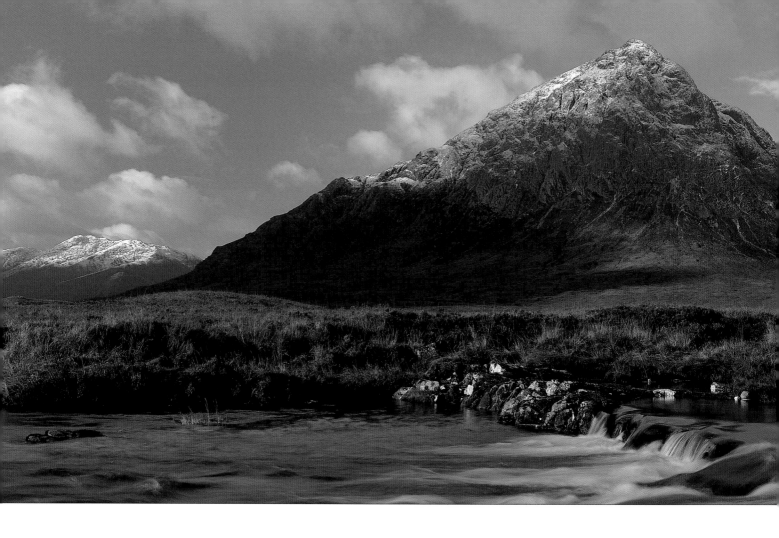

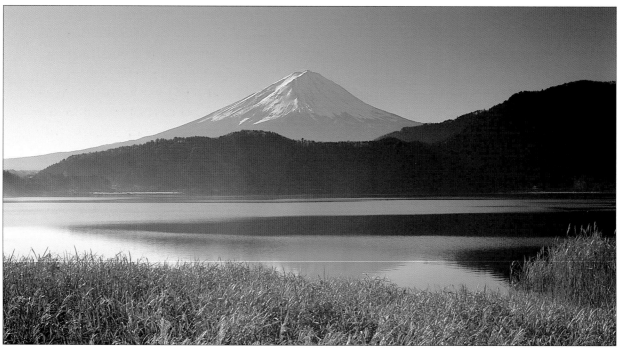

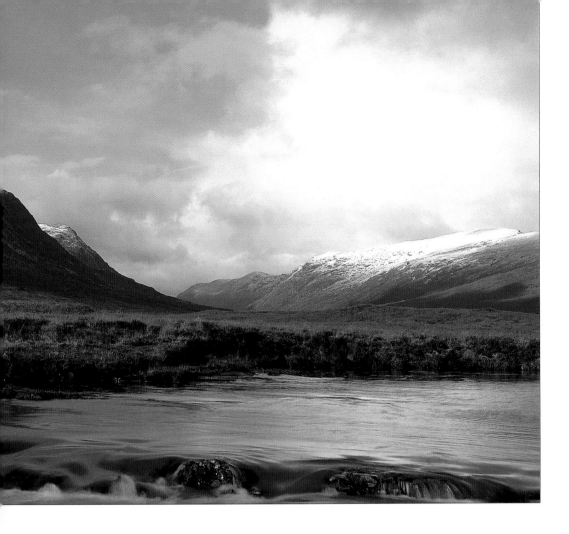

MOUNT FUJI AND REFLECTION

I spent a day viewing Fuji from every angle. I like the combination of the soft, silky surface of the water and the hard, conical mountain. The bright orange vegetation in the foreground is a startling contrast to the predominantly cool blues of the rest of the image. I believe that reflections should be included in their entirety where possible, otherwise the image looks unconsidered and badly executed. I didn't have a ladder so, sadly, the top of the reflection is nicked by the foreground.

Location: MOUNT FUJI, JAPAN

Camera: 6cm x 6cm; Lens: 50mm; Film: Fuji 50 ASA; Exposure: ¼ second at f.22; Filter: polarizing

BUCHAILLETIVE

I trudged through bog to get this view of Buchailletive, which shows the mountain at its most pyramid-like – it looks entirely different from other angles. I liked the symmetry of the conical peak and hoped that shadows would turn its lower slopes obsidian black. It rained at least half a dozen times, and on each occasion I had to retreat with my equipment under a tarpaulin. The side lighting picks out the fissures and serrations on the surface, the dusting of snow on the peak, and the golden ocher platform on which the mountain appears to sit.

Location: BUCHAILLETIVE, SCOTLAND

Camera: 6cm x 17cm (cropped image); Lens: 105 mm; Film: Fuji 50 ASA; Exposure: 1 second at f.64; Filter: polarizing

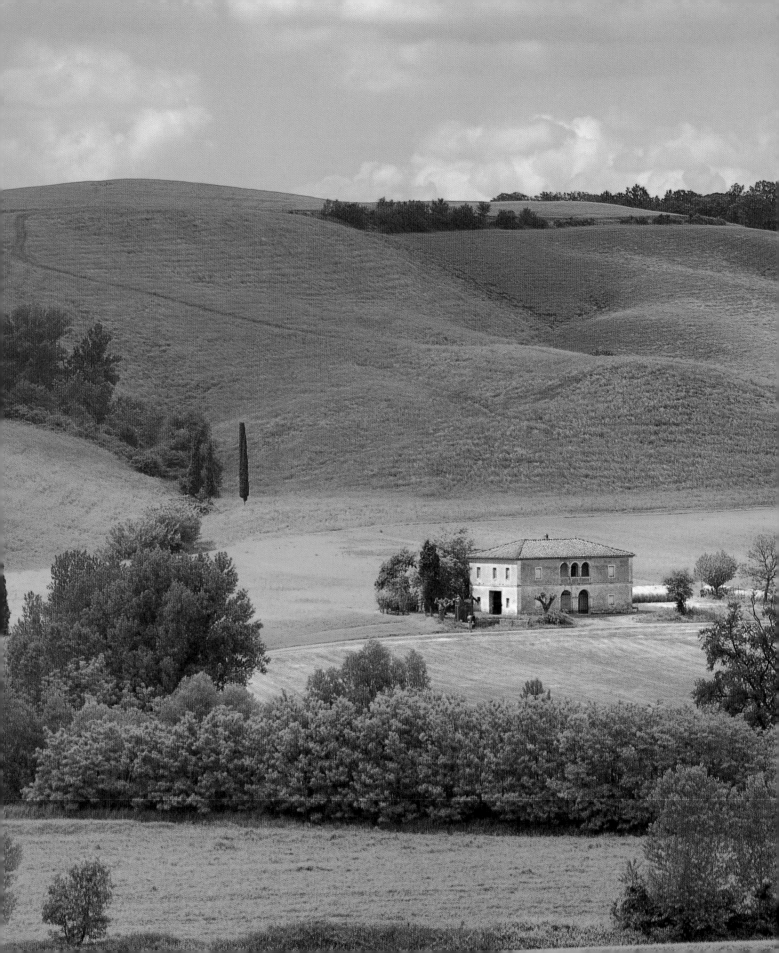

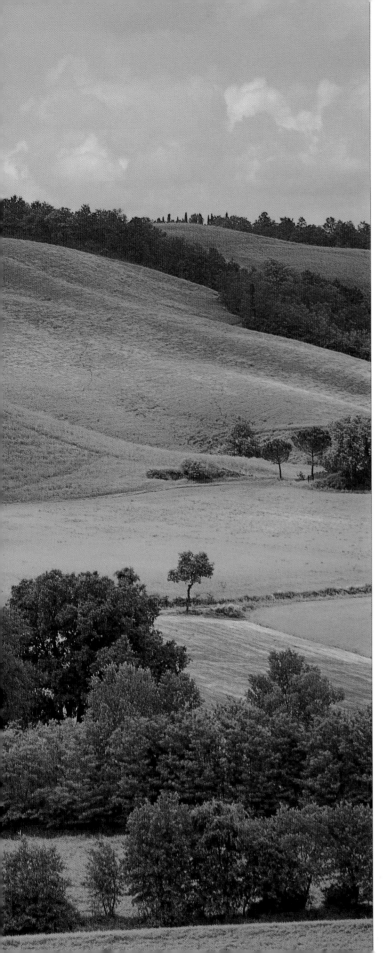

The Landscape as Backdrop

The landscape provides a context for many human activities, from agricultural tasks like ploughing and harvesting, to everyday chores like cooking, going to market, or chopping wood. It is also the setting for manmade structures, from grand houses to rustic barns, snaking roads, canals, and bridges. The landscape photographer must find a way of making these elements sit comfortably within their context, so that one enhances the other.

HARMONIOUS COLORS

I have often seen this mellow, pink villa from the road, but I had to search out this vantage point. The afternoon light was gentle and diffuse but there was enough contrast and the house was nicely spotlit. I like its symmetry, and the way it is set on an apron of stubble, which resonates with the colors of the stonework and contrasts with the greens. The sky with its half-hearted cloud is a little weak.

Location: TUSCANY, ITALY

Camera: 6cm x 6cm; Lens: 150mm;
Film: Fuji 50 ASA; Exposure: ⅟₁₅ second at f.16

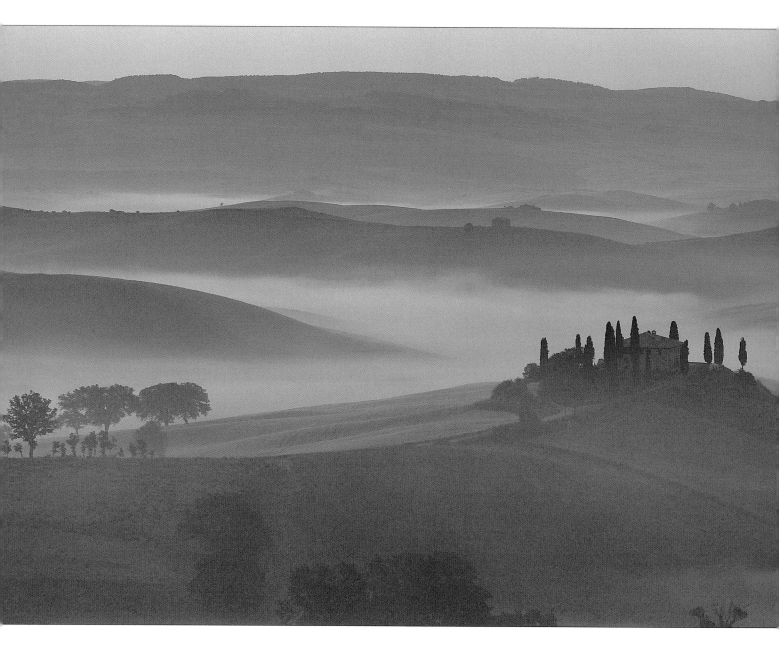

TUSCAN DAWN

Rain at nightfall often produces sublime effects at sunrise. At 5:00 AM the mist was eddying like veils of chiffon, and by 5:15 AM the sky was taking on a pinkish blush. Presented with such a cavalcade of effects I always take a sequence of photographs – but I am pretty sure at that time which is 'the one'. I love the combination of softness and crispness, the diffuse light behind the shapes, and the way small elements, like the trees, become very strong.

Location: TUSCANY, ITALY

Camera: 6cm x 17cm; Lens: 300mm; Film: Fuji 50 ASA;
Exposure: 8 seconds at f.64: Filter: polarizer

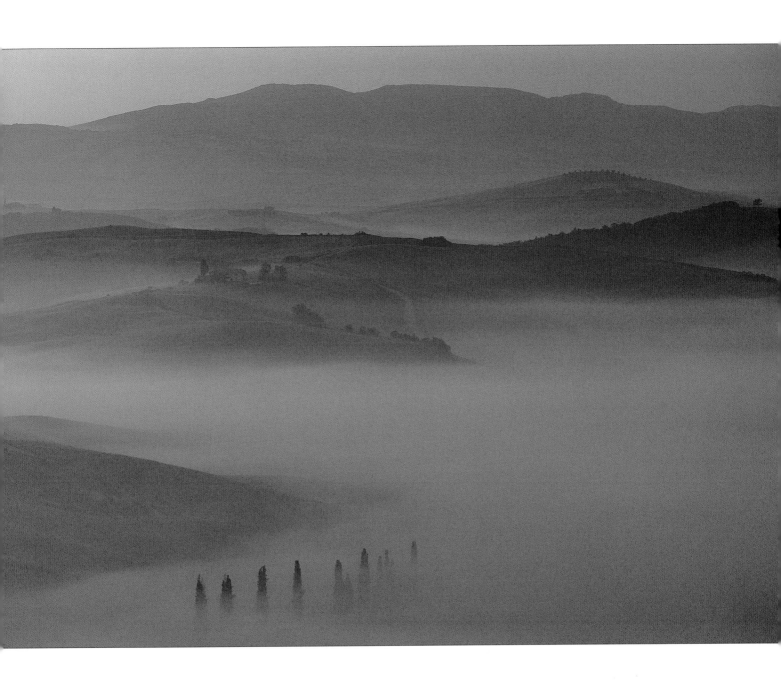

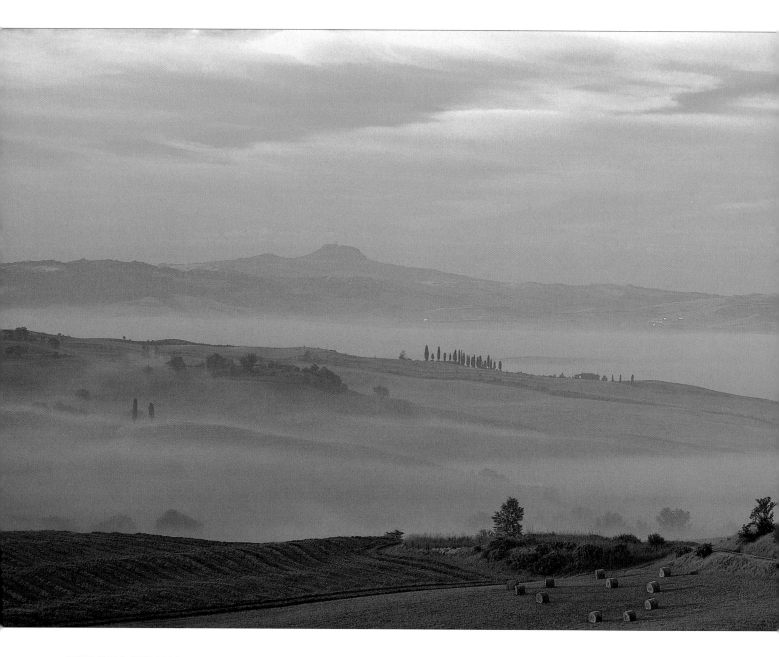

TUSCAN SUNRISE

Things happen at dawn that only very early risers normally see. In this period of transition the landscape is totally transformed for a very short time and then it all becomes familiar again. Here the sun has gilded the walls of the villa, and also the bales of hay, which look like modern sculptures. Ten minutes later the whole thing was over and we came crashing back to reality.

Location: TUSCANY, ITALY

Camera: 6cm x 17cm; Lens: 300mm; Film: Fuji 50 ASA;
Exposure: 2 seconds at f.64; Filter: polarizer

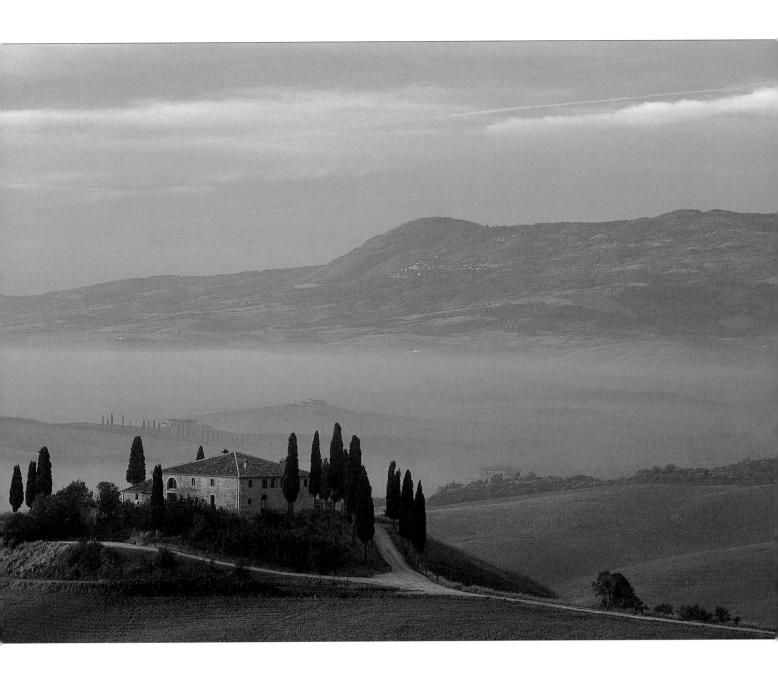

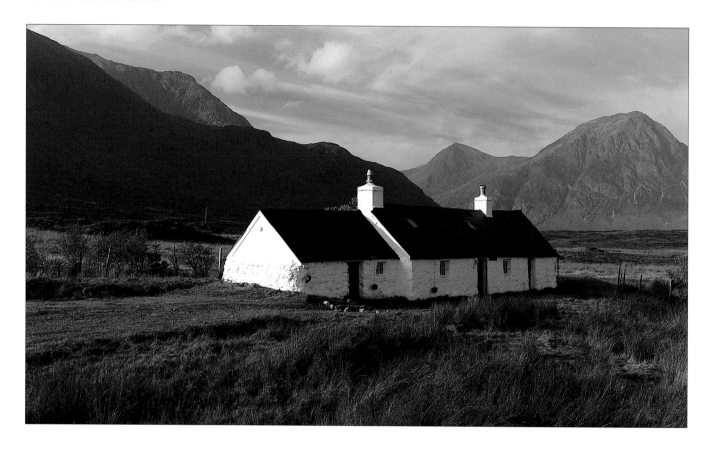

BLACK ROCK COTTAGE, ISOLATED

This bothy on Rannoch Moor is beautiful, remote, and much photographed. I have framed the picture to make the mountains fold in behind the white cottage, and ensured that the chimneys don't break the line of the mountains. The slope of the roofs mirrors the slope of the mountains, which makes for a satisfying composition. The sky is not very interesting and ultraviolet light has made the shaded walls appear blue.

Location: RANNOCH MOOR, SCOTLAND

Camera: 6cm x 6cm; Lens: 50mm;
Film: Fuji 50 ASA; Exposure: ⅟₃₀ second at f.11

BLACK ROCK COTTAGE, IN CONTEXT

This version was taken 15 years ago. The cottage sits back into the hill behind, creating a unity with the landscape. Warmer light counteracts the bluishness evident in the alternative photograph. The house is not receiving direct light, so the mood is more gentle and romantic – the bit of mist in the background helps. The deep foreground with its interesting clumps of vegetation and rocks emphasizes the remoteness of the cottage.

Location: RANNOCH MOOR, SCOTLAND

Camera: 6cm x 6cm; Lens: 50mm;
Film: Fuji 50 ASA; Exposure: ⅟₁₅ second at f.11–16

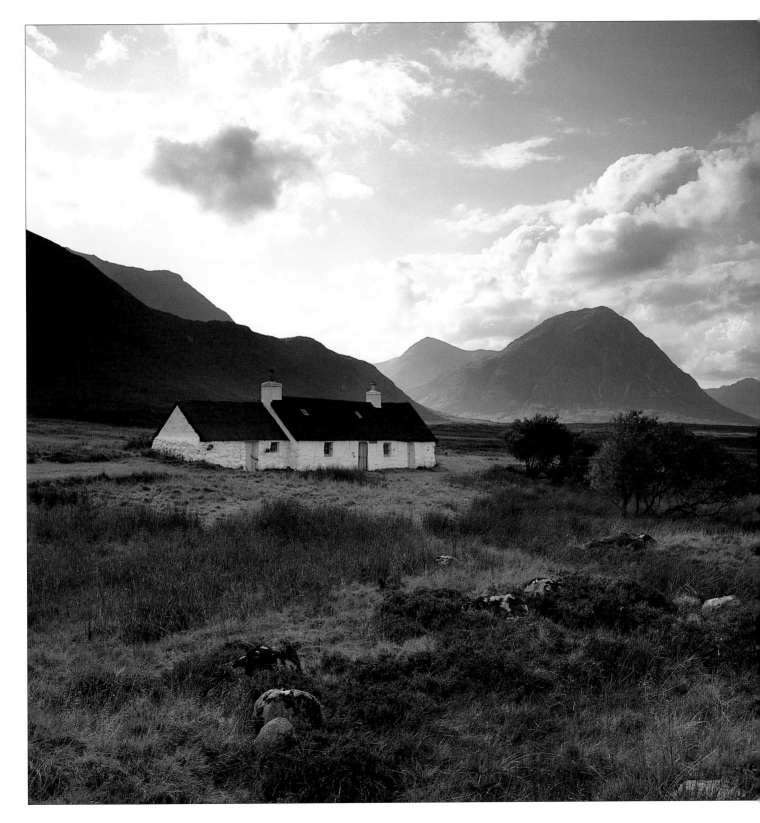

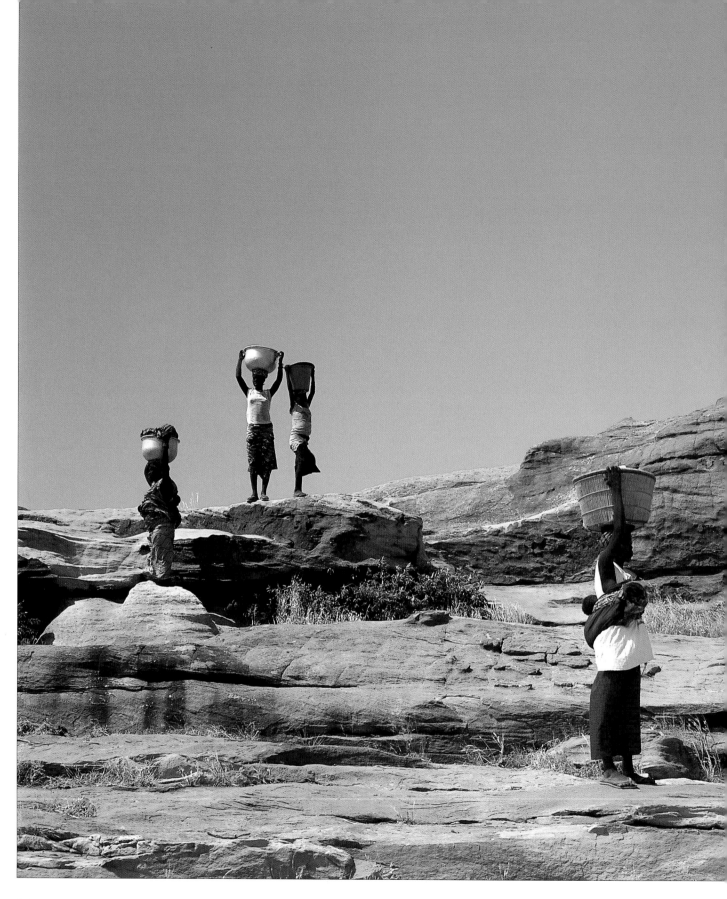

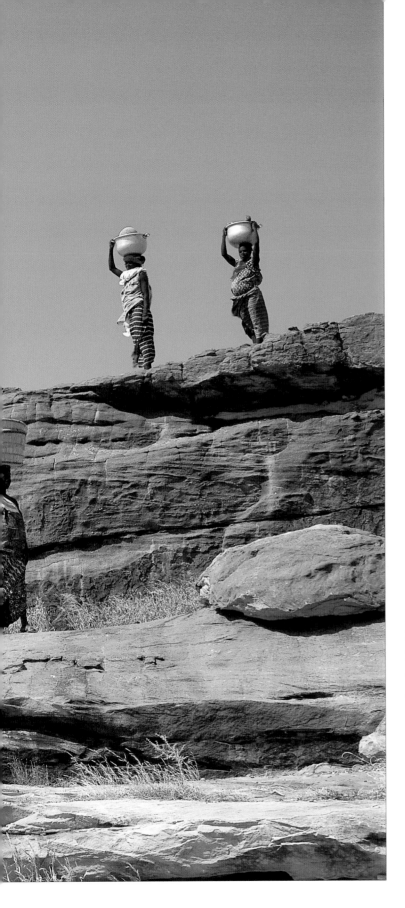

DOGON GOING TO MARKET

I came across these people as they made their way to the local market and asked if I might photograph them. I took them more or less as they were with only a little arrangement. Their graceful stance, the lovely colors and patterns of their clothing, and the silvery surface of their aluminium pots make a pleasing contract with the bare sandstone. The scattered figures are like exclamation marks against the landscape.

Location: MALI, AFRICA

Camera: 6cm x 6cm; Lens: 150mm;
Film: Fuji 50 ASA; Exposure: 1/30 second at f.11

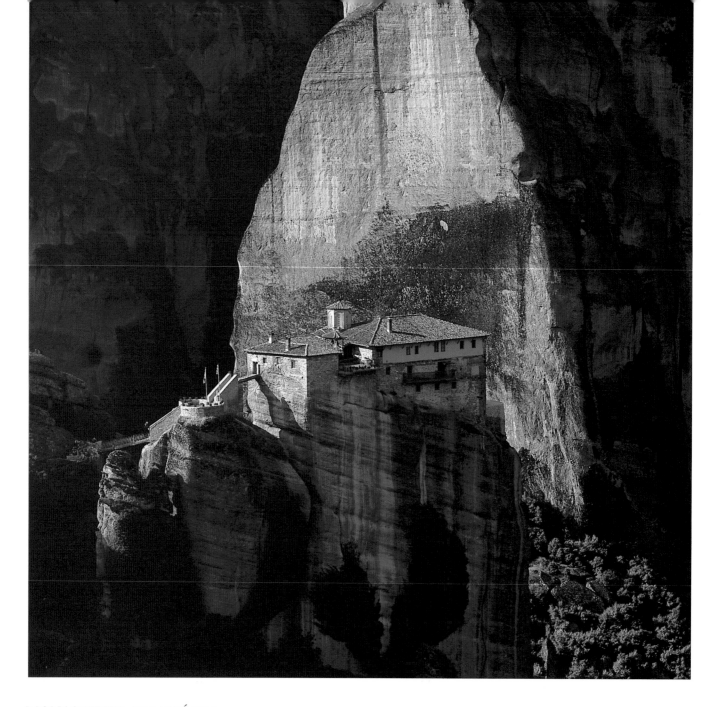

MONASTERIES AT METÉORA

A beam of light from the right glances across the buildings and delivers its full force onto the rockface, which is the backdrop to this tableau. It reveals delicate hues – mauve, blue-green, and primrose – and an intricately weathered surface. At first glance the image is ambiguous because the monastery itself is 80% in shadow, and the lit areas create an abstract shape.

Location: METÉORA, GREECE

Camera: 6cm x 6cm; Lens: 150mm; Film: Fuji 100 ASA;
Exposure: 1 second at f.32; Filters: polarizer, 81B (warm up)

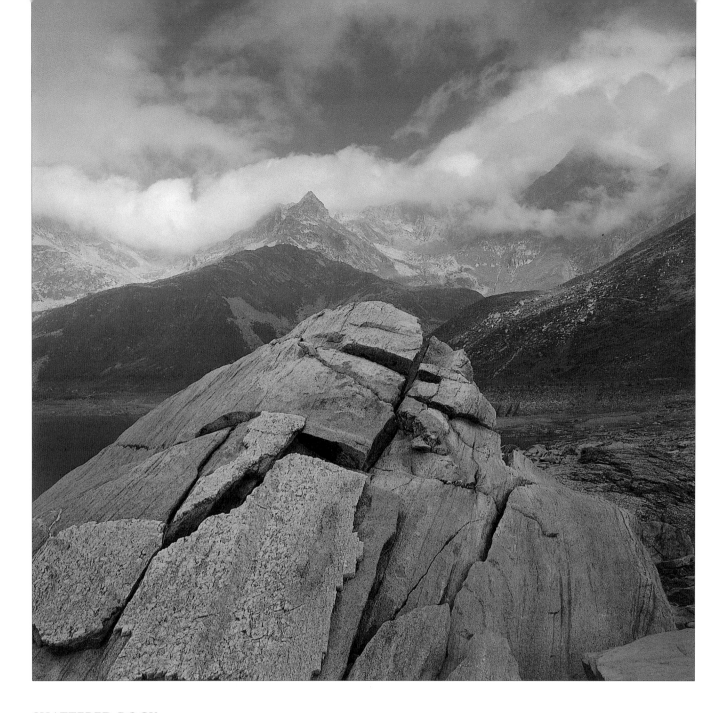

SHATTERED ROCK

This frost-shattered rock has the strangeness of a piece of contemporary sculpture. It was cold and overcast, and the mountains kept disappearing under blanketing cloud. I was beginning to despair of making a photograph work when a short walk brought me to this spot. The colors, shapes, and textures of the rock mimic those of the mountains behind, while its fissures and fractures are a powerful evocation of the forces that created them.

Location: LOMBARDY, ITALY

Camera: 6cm x 6cm; Lens: 50mm; Film: Fuji 50 ASA; Exposure: 2 seconds at f.22

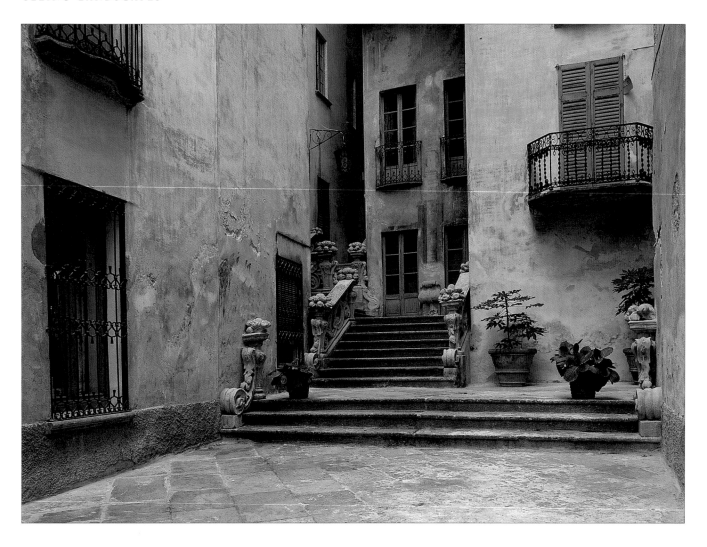

ALL THE WORLD'S A STAGE

This is one of my favorite photographs. It captures the stillness of a stage set before the players appear – it even has a Romeo-and-Juliet-style balcony. It was raining and the soft, even light was kind to the muted pinks and pearly grays of weathered plaster and peeling paint. Sunshine would have created distracting splashes of bright light. The only irritant is the red sign by the upper-right window.

Location: LOMBARDY, ITALY

Camera: 6cm x 6cm; Lens: 50mm;
Film: Fuji 50 ASA; Exposure: 1 second at f.22

VITAL DETAILS

This could also be a stage set propped with the tools of a barber's trade. Each element in this tableau is important to the owner – the towels, the flask, and the well-worn kettle and aluminium pots. I love the out-of-date calendar and the poster of hair styles that no one could possibly want. Although it is much busier than most of my photographs, the sheer abundance of detail and the closely related colors and tones come together to make a satisfying whole.

Location: DALI, CHINA

Camera: 6cm x 6cm; Lens: 50mm;
Film: Fuji 50 ASA; Exposure: ⅛ second at f.11

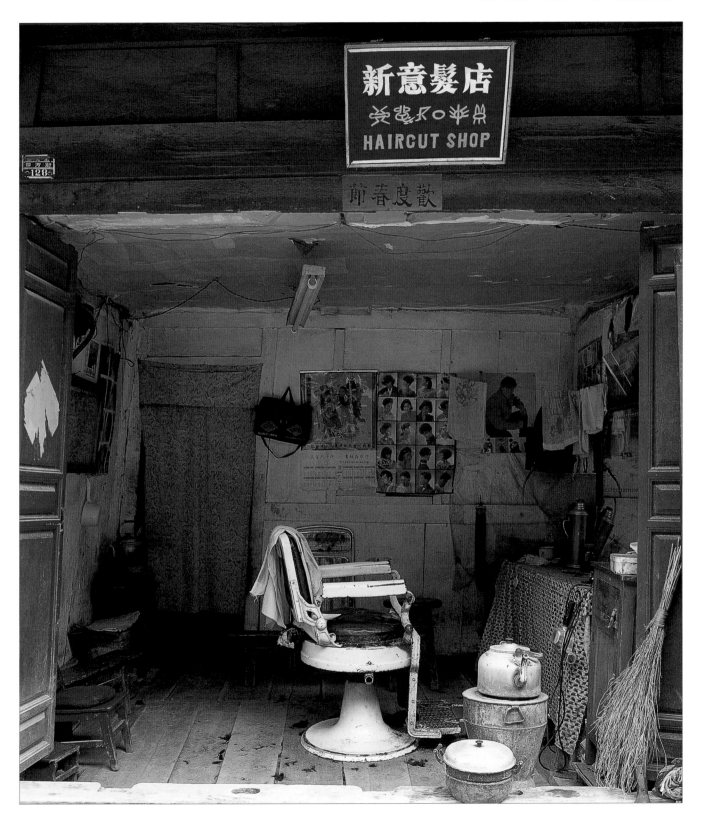

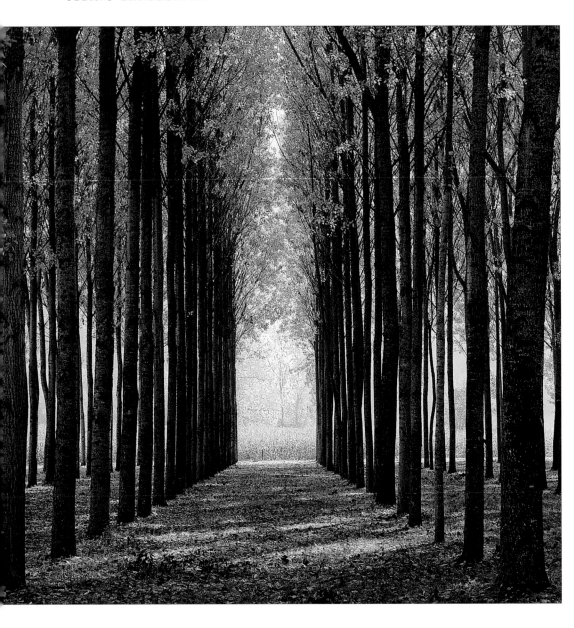

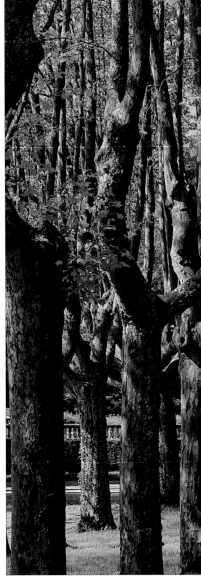

KEEPING THE VERTICALS

The avenues within this plantation evoked the aisles of a Gothic cathedral, and the light looked as if it was spilling through stained glass. I wandered around until I found the location with the precision and the contained feeling that I wanted, and spent time getting the correct viewpoint. It was important that the tree bases converged at the same angle, that the end opening was central, and that the verticals did not converge.

Location: DORDOGNE, FRANCE

Camera: 6cm x 6cm; Lens: 80mm; Film: Kodak 64 ASA; Exposure: ½ second at f.32

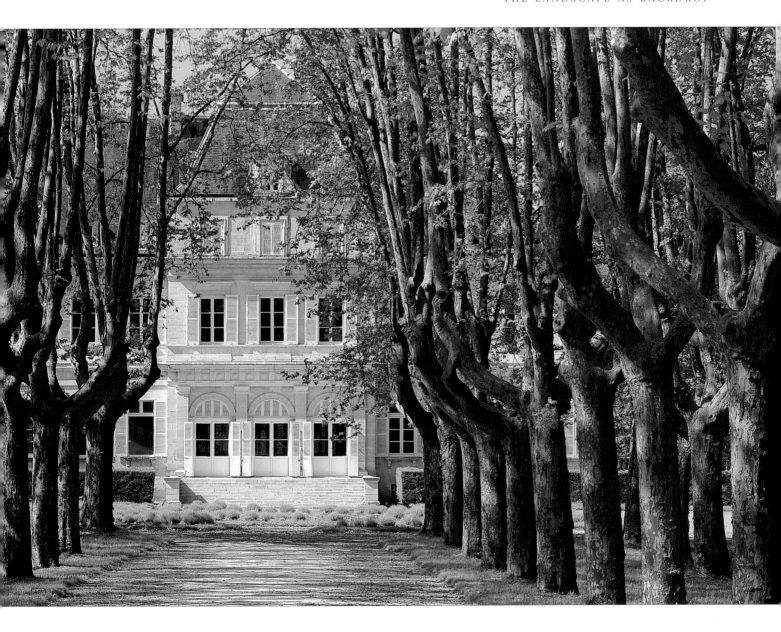

IN THE FRAME

I glimpsed this avenue of trees leading to an elegant chateau and was determined to photograph it. Returning at the same time – 8:00 AM – on the following day, I found the gates padlocked and the windows shuttered. But a caretaker appeared, unlocked the gates, threw open the shutters, and I got my picture.

Location: THE LOT, FRANCE

Camera: 6cm x 17cm, cropped image; Lens: 300mm;
Film: Fuji 50 ASA; Exposure: 2 seconds at f.64; Filter: polarizer

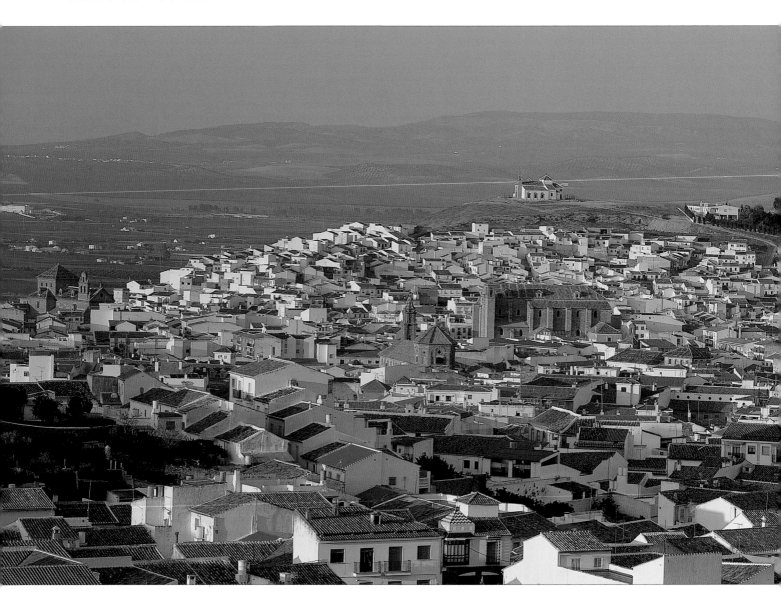

CUBIST VIEW

This jumble of dwellings reminds me of a cubist image, with lots of planes butted up against each other. Although the town is sidelit there are few deep shadows because the buildings are white, and light is reflected off the opposing walls of the adjacent houses. Some of the shadows have a warm, pinkish tinge, which links to the color of the rooftops. A viewpoint from which you can see across the roofs of a town has great photographic potential.

Location: ANDALUSIA, SPAIN

Camera: 6cm x 17cm; Lens: 300mm; Film: Fuji 50 ASA;
Exposure: 1 second at f.45; Filters: polarizer, 81C (warm up)

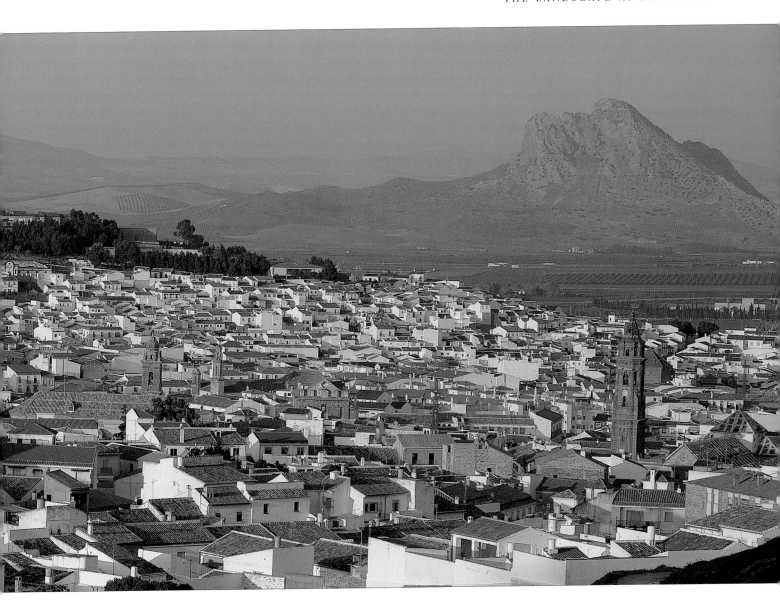

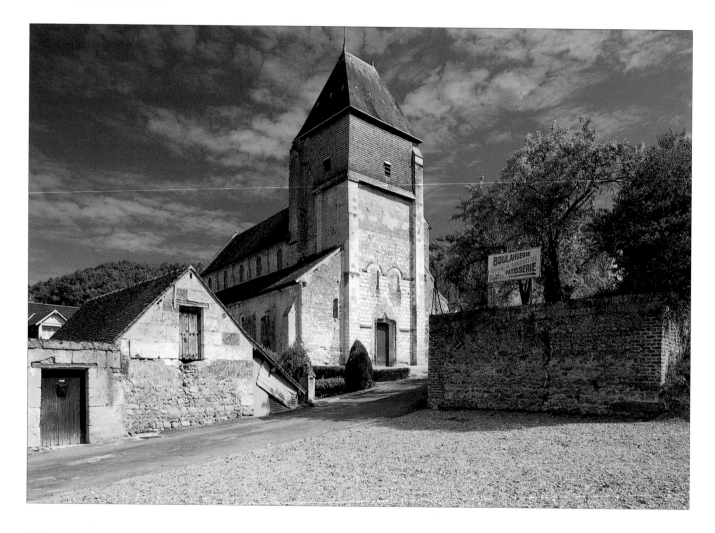

TOWERING FOCAL POINT: 1

The gravel in the foreground echoes the creamy tones of
the buildings and the low viewpoint makes the tower look
imposing. The sky is crucial – the fluffy clouds modify
the blue and create a sense of recession. I used a ladder to
compensate for convergence but couldn't quite stop the
tower from tipping over. The blank wall on the right is
saved by the boulangerie sign with its lovely typography.
Unfortunately, the finial at the top of the tower is nicking
the edge of the frame – I couldn't quite get it in.

Location: LOIRE, FRANCE

Camera: 6cm x 6cm; Lens: 50mm; Film: Kodak 64 ASA;
Exposure: ⅛ second at f.22; Filters: polarizer, 81A (warm up)

TOWERING FOCAL POINT: 2

A little light can go a long way. In this evocative scene,
most of the image is devoid of light. The muted background provides a marvellous foil for the everyday 'story'
below. The tiniest slivers of light sneak into the lower part
of the picture, creating a rim light around the elderly
lady's hair and shoulder, and illuminating the duck's white
plumage. The diagonals of slanting shadows underline the
little drama and tug you toward that part of the picture.

Location: DORDOGNE, FRANCE

Camera: 35mm; Lens: 200mm; Film: Fuji 100 ASA;
Exposure: 1/30 second at f.11–16; Filter: 81A (warm up)

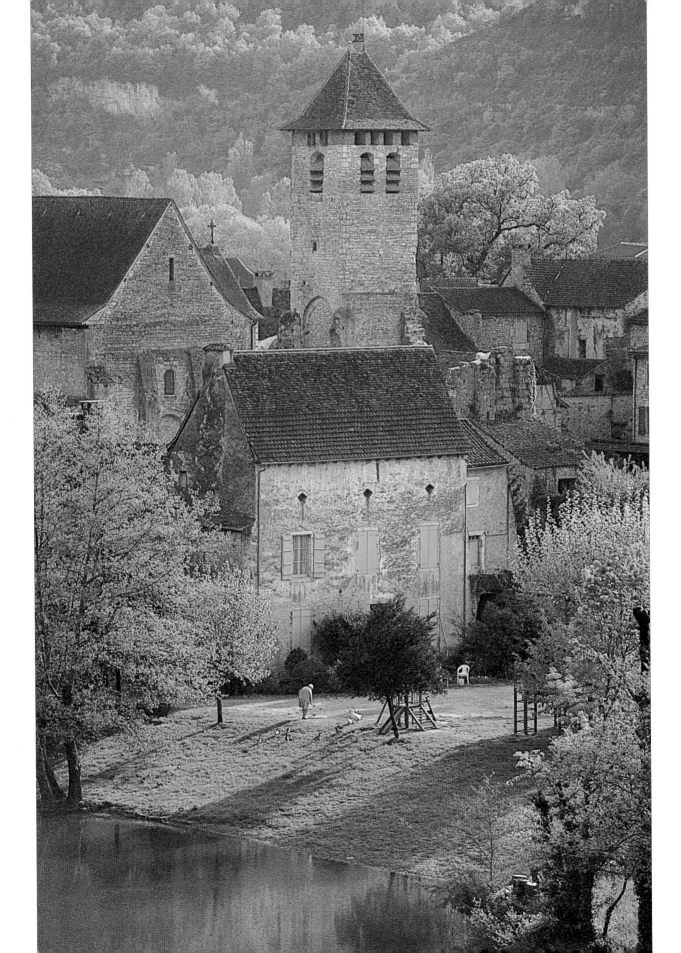

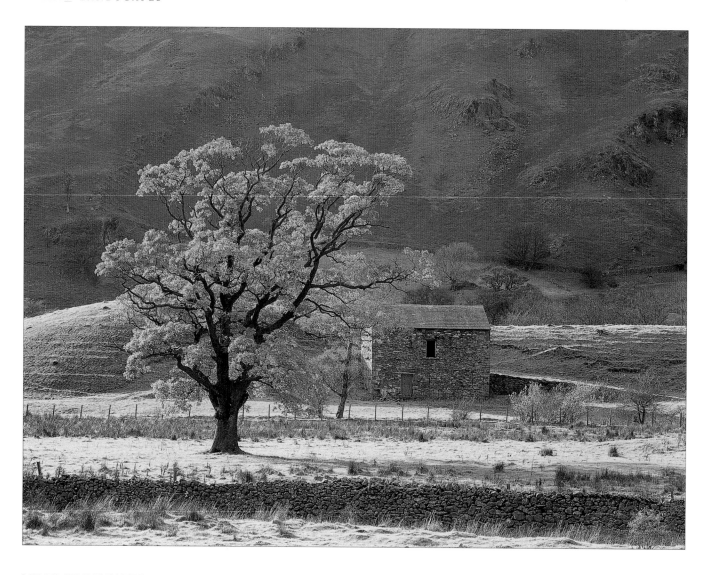

NEAR ULLSWATER

The solitary barn looked inviting and homely. The colors and textures of the hill seemed the perfect foil. The walls and shadows provide good horizontals, which are balanced by the vertical young oak tree with its snaking black branches and crinkly foliage. The hill is in shadow, which gives the image a contained feeling, and emphasizes the shafts of bright light and dark shadow in the foreground.

Location: CUMBRIA, ENGLAND

Camera: 6cm x 6cm; Lens: 150mm; Film: Fuji 50 ASA; Exposure: ⅟₁₅ second at f.11–16; Filter: polarizer

FIVE SECONDS LATER

One minute the sky was overcast, the next bright light was brushing across the hills. Trying to anticipate what would happen next and deciding when to take the picture is often tantalizing. I was there for between one and two hours but these pictures were taken five seconds apart. Here, a more general light plays up the colors and textures, and, as the sky is included, the image feels open and airy.

Location: CUMBRIA, ENGLAND

Camera: 6cm x 6cm; Lens: 150mm; Film: Fuji 50 ASA; Exposure: ⅟₁₅ second at f.11

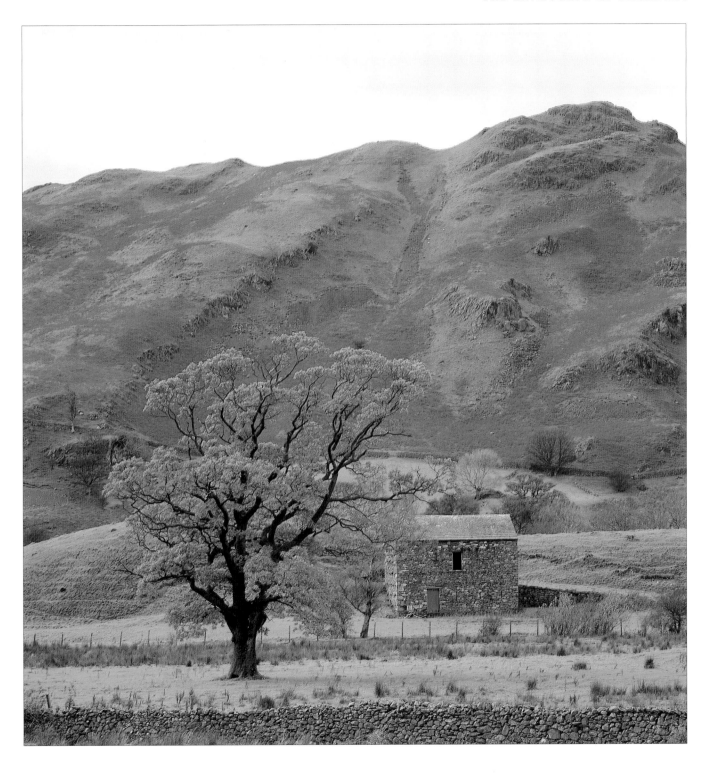

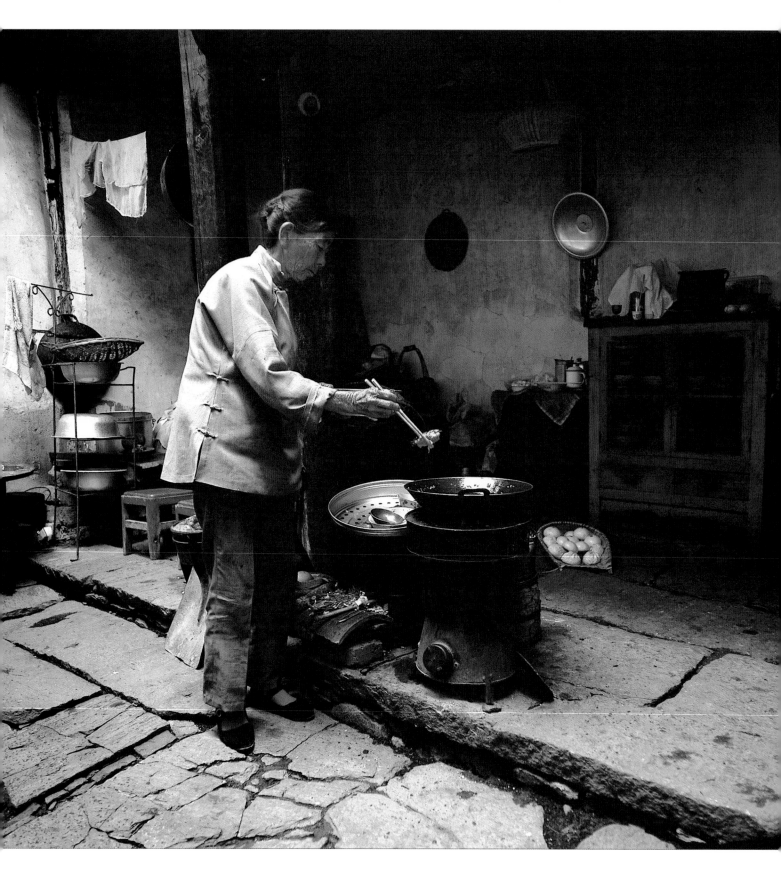

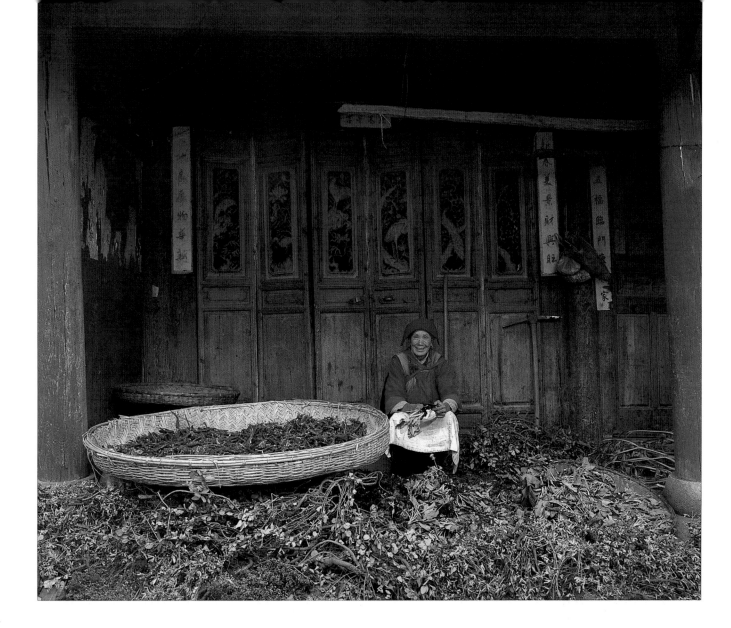

PERFECTLY PROPPED

I came across this scene in a courtyard. Everything in the composition seemed considered, from the crease in the woman's trousers to the colors in the kitchen. This photograph encourages your eye to roam around and discover details such as the reflections on her cookware. The cool, muted colors counteract the busy-ness of the subject.

Location: HIZOU, CHINA

Camera: 6cm x 6cm; Lens: 10mm;
Film: Fuji 400 ASA; Exposure: ⅛ second at f.11

MRS HO

Mrs Ho was sitting on a stool preparing plants for her husband's herbal medicines. The carved panels create a magnificent set for the tiny lady, while the basket dwarfs her. Rain made the light soft – if it had been brighter some areas would have been plunged into dark, concealing shadow. I loved her radiant smile.

Location: BAISHA, CHINA

Camera: 6cm x 6cm; Lens: 50mm;
Film: Fuji 50 ASA; Exposure: ¼ second at f.22

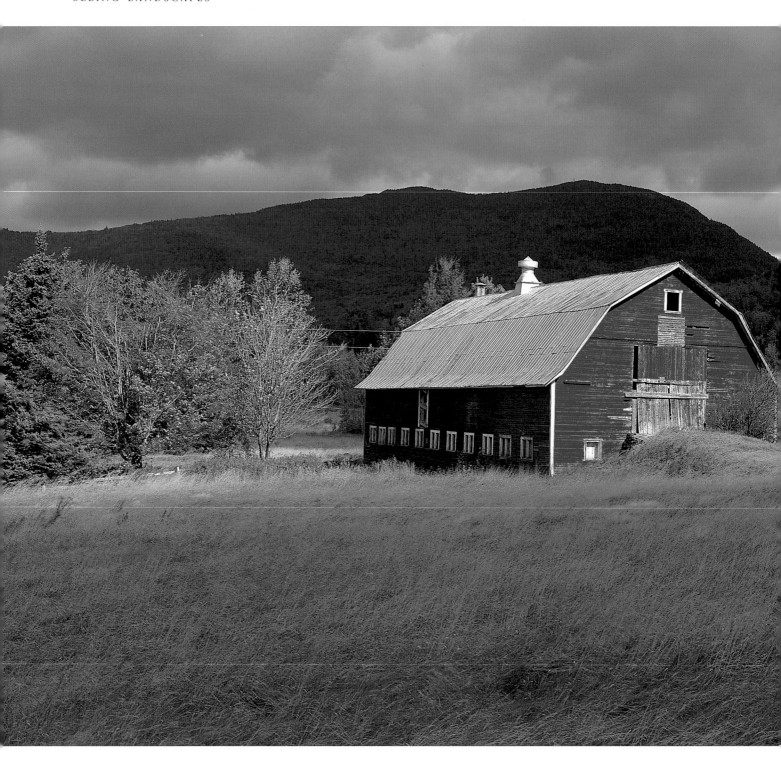

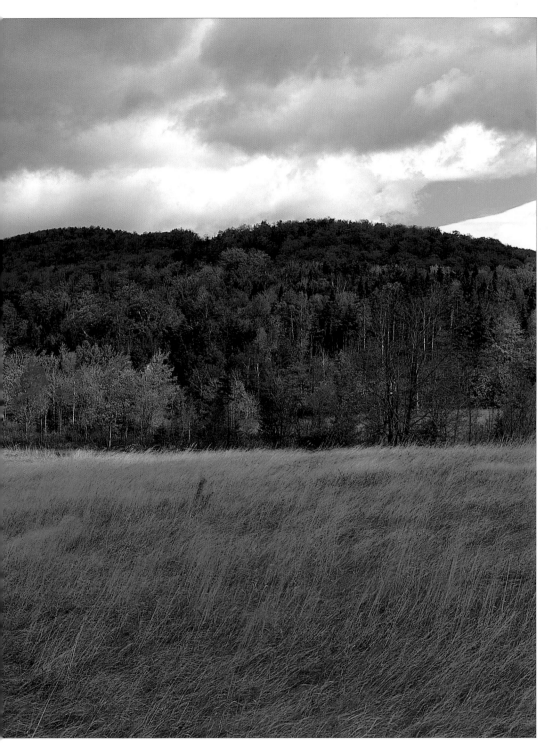

CENTER STAGE

The eye naturally seeks out similarities in a picture and here the hipped roof echoes the shape of the hill behind. From the road the top of the barn bisected the skyline but by scrambling up the slope I was able to tuck it under the hill. It is not a beautiful building and when I arrived it was unlit and dead. I waited for two hours to get just the right light on the building, the darkened foreground, and shadow on the hills. It's great when a long wait finally pays off.

Location: VERMONT, USA

Camera: 6cm x 17cm;
Lens: 105mm;
Film: Fuji 50 ASA;
Exposure: $\frac{1}{60}$ second at f.45;
Filter: polarizer

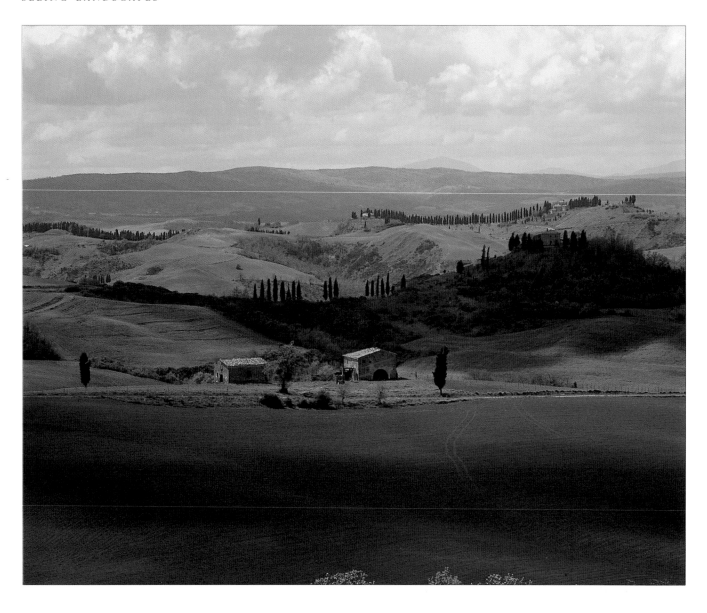

TWO BARNS IN TUSCANY: SUMMER

This is a familiar and frequently visited location, and these photographs were taken years apart and at different times of the year. In this version there is a big, deep landscape, although the barns with their brightly lit roofs are certainly the focus. The overlapping planes recede into the background, with a chocolaty brown in the foreground, passing through shades of green to the blue-green of the distant hills and the pale, cloud-filled sky.

Location: TUSCANY, ITALY

Camera: 6cm x 6cm; Lens: 80mm; Film: Kodak 64 ASA;
Exposure: 1/60 second at f.8; Filters: polarizer, 81B (warm up)

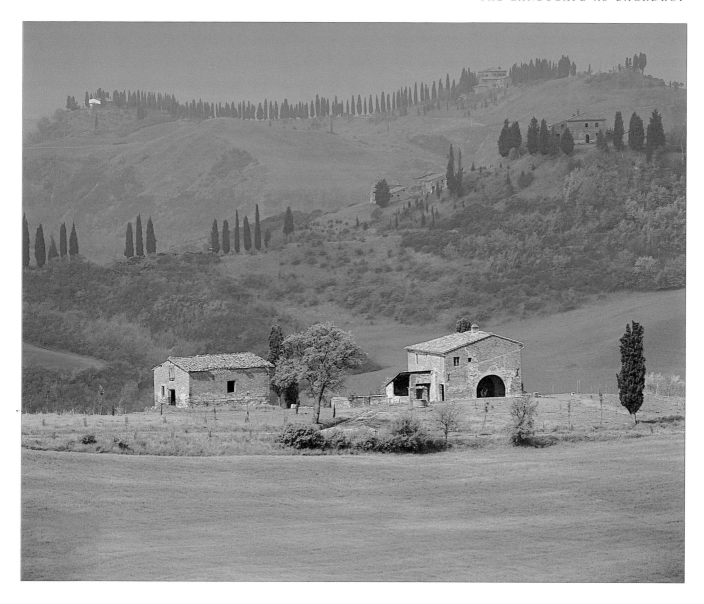

TWO BARNS IN TUSCANY: SPRING

Here, there is a much shallower picture area. A different viewpoint brings the hill in the middle-distance forward, so it closes the picture area. This puts the row of trees onto the skyline – like decorative finials. The range of colors seems more coherent, and by cropping out the sky attention is focused on the barns. These qualities, and the more graphic feel, make it a more pleasing image. The foreground grass provides a useful platform.

Location: TUSCANY, ITALY

Camera: 6cm x 6cm; Lens: 250mm; Film: Fuji 50 ASA;
Exposure: ⅓₀ second at f.8–11; Filters: polarizer, 81A (warm up)

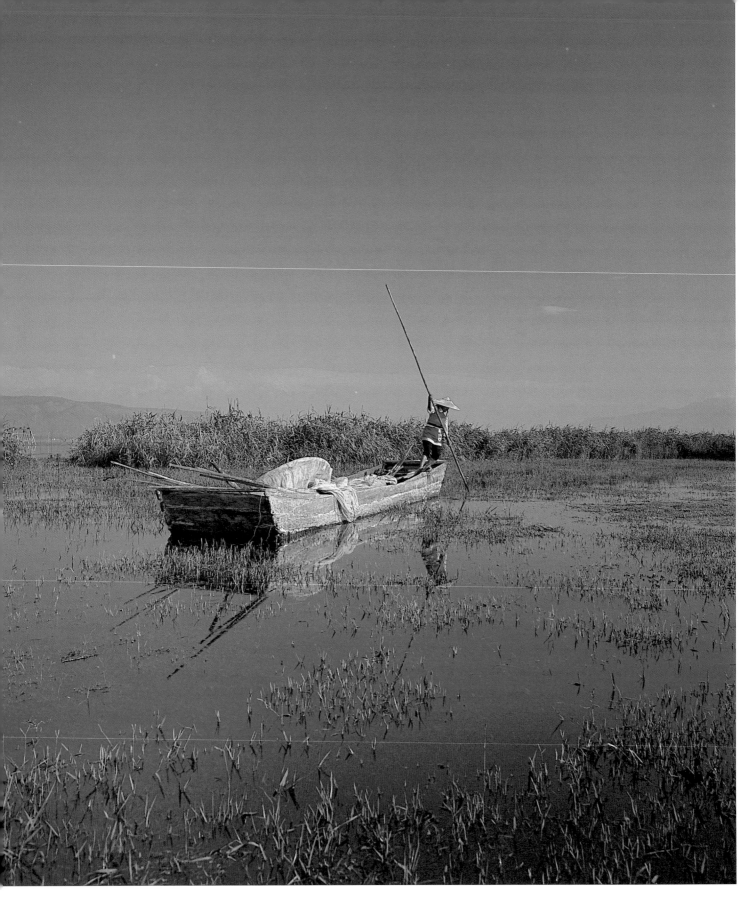

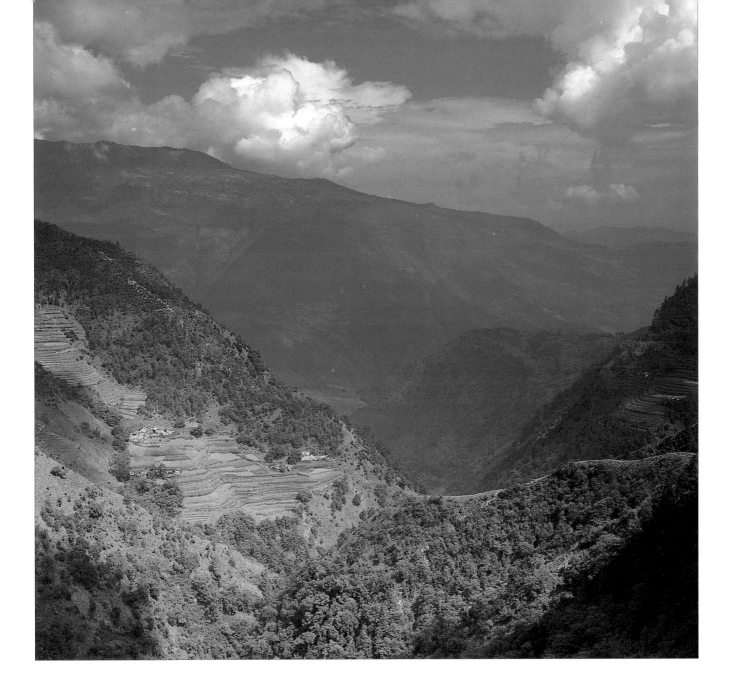

SIMPLIFYING THE SCENE

By eliminating extraneous detail I have created a simple composition. Taking a low viewpoint I split the image into one-half sky and one-half water. The angles of the punt and its reflections are counterbalanced by the pole, the only element that projects into the upper half.

Location: DALI, CHINA

Camera: 6cm x 6cm; Lens: 50mm;
Film: Fuji 50 ASA; Exposure: 1/30 second at f.8–11

FLEETING LIGHT

I looked for terracing because it instantly signifies the orient. This is an awesome landscape with towering mountains, sheer-sided valleys, and terraced paddy fields. The wind was blowing the clouds at phenomenal speed, so I had to work quickly to grab the illumination I required.

Location: LIJIANG, CHINA

Camera: 6cm x 6cm; Lens: 80mm;
Film: Fuji 50 ASA; Exposure: 1/30 second at f.8–11

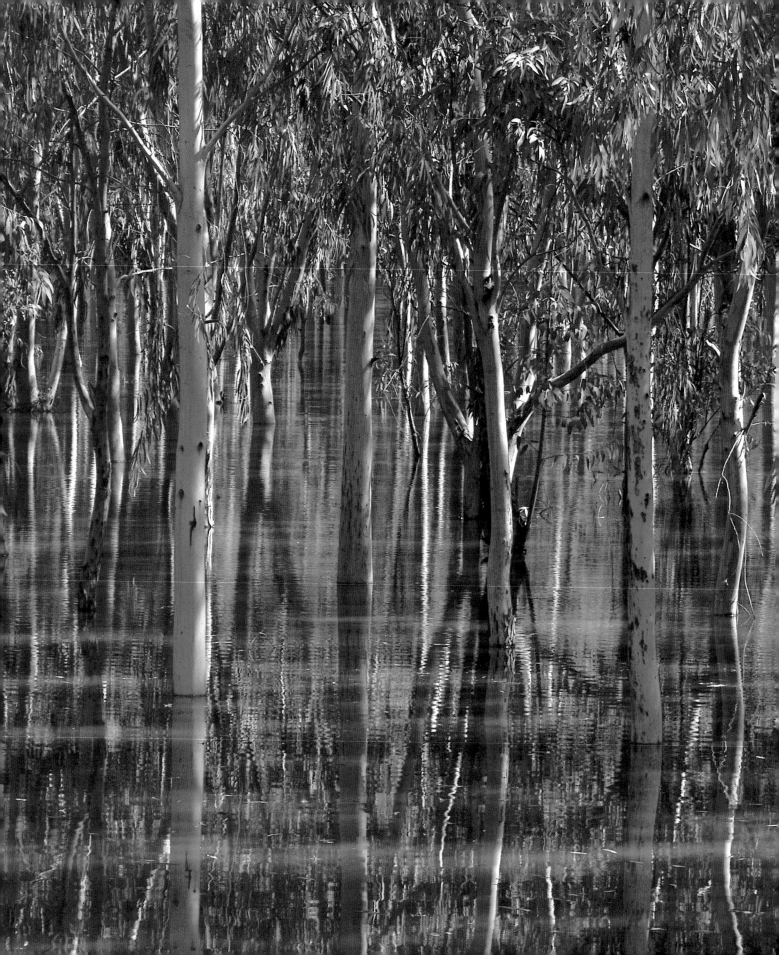

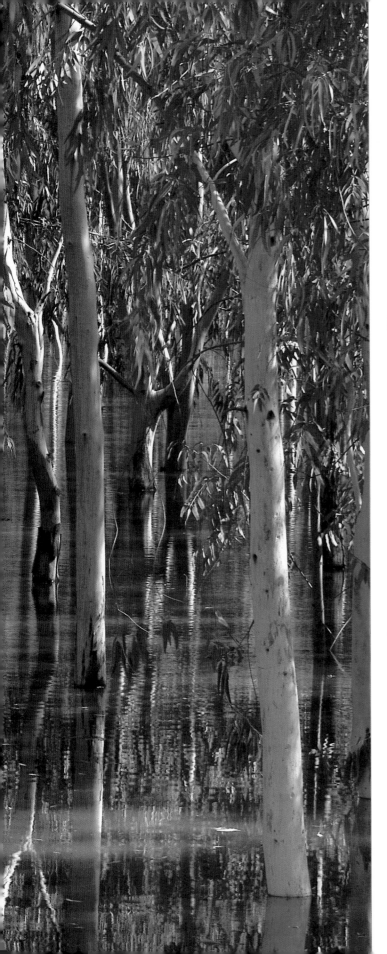

Approaches to the Landscape

A landscape photograph may be a literal description of a scene or a more creative and personal interpretation. A landscape can become an abstract arrangement of colors, tones, and textures or a decorative pattern of repeating shapes. While some images are gentle, others have a theatrical quality. By selecting the subject and exploiting the light you can produce an image that has the qualities of an impressionist painting, or create a surreal image.

TOWARD ABSTRACTION

Gum trees reflected in flood waters produce an image that hovers between precise description and abstraction. In the foreground the verticals of six trees are easy to discern and their reflections are well defined. These trees dictate a kind of order. Behind them a cohesive confusion of trunks, leaves, water, and reflections form a backcloth of light, dark, and shades of green. There is little to focus on in that area, so the image resolves and dissolves in a tantalizing way.

Location: MALI, AFRICA

Camera: 6cm x 6cm; Lens: 150mm;
Film: Fuji 50 ASA; Exposure: 1 second at f.32

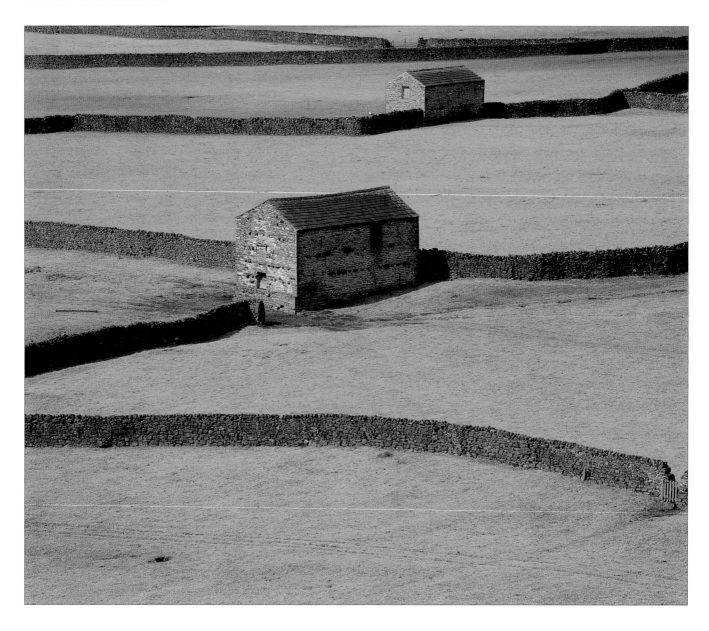

SIMPLE GEOMETRY

I find the simple geometry of these walls very pleasing. I isolated this segment as it had simplicity and clarity, and the walls produced an internal dynamic that leads the eye around and over the image. Despite the change of scale between the barns, the image has little depth, which emphasizes its abstract qualities.

Location: YORKSHIRE, ENGLAND

Camera: 6cm x 6cm; Lens: 250mm; Film: Fuji 50 ASA;
Exposure: ¼ second at f.32; Filter: 81A (warm up)

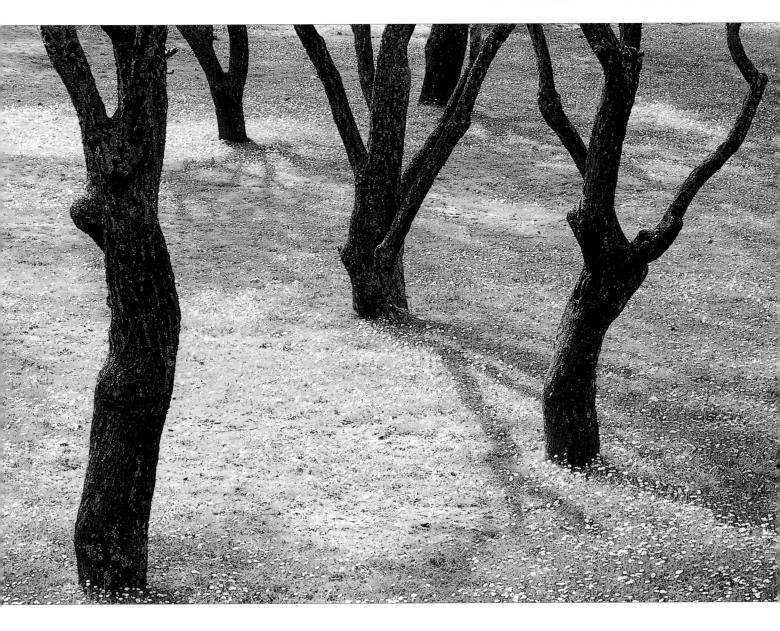

NEGATIVE IMPACT

I had to balance on crumbly walls to get a viewpoint where each tree was isolated but they were not masking each other. There is one intruding trunk at the back. I had little latitude – the position had to be exact. I cropped to focus on the dark trunks against crisp light and the 'negative' shapes between the branches. The daisies break up the solidity of the grass.

Location: Turkey

Camera: 6cm x 6cm; Lens: 150mm; Film: Fuji 50 ASA;
Exposure: 1 second at f.32; Filter: polarizer, 50%

121

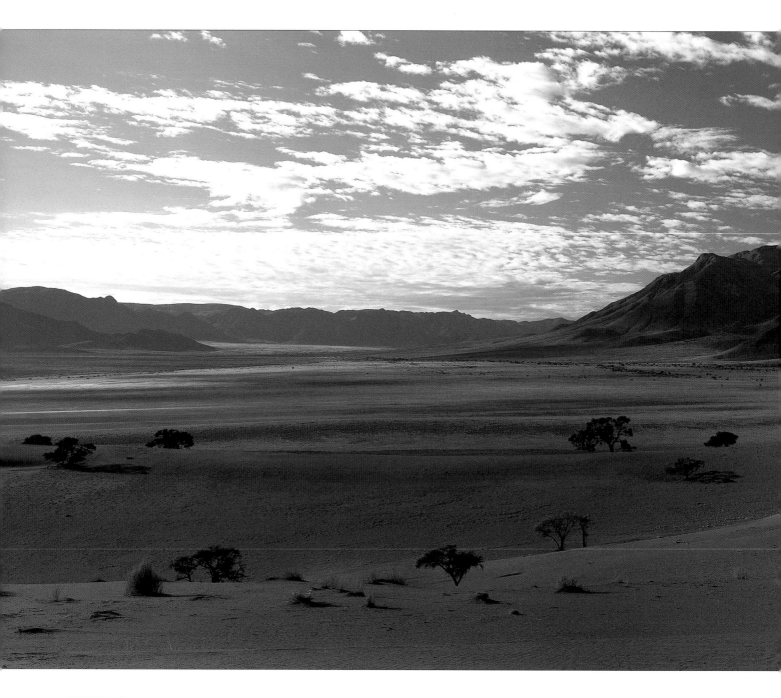

KEEPING THE FOCUS

A formidable mountain provides a strong foil for the vast sweep of sand in the foreground, punctuated by trees. Within ten minutes of the photograph being taken, the clouds had evaporated and the cohesion of the picture had disintegrated.

Location: NAMIBIA, AFRICA

Camera: 6cm x 17cm; Lens: 105mm; Film: Fuji 50 ASA;
Exposure: 3 seconds at f.64; Filter: polarizer

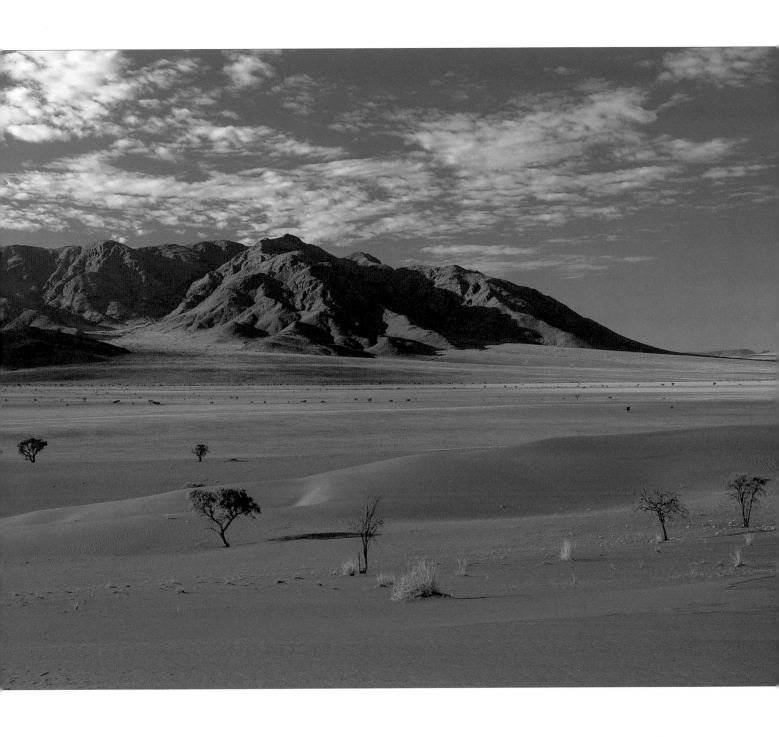

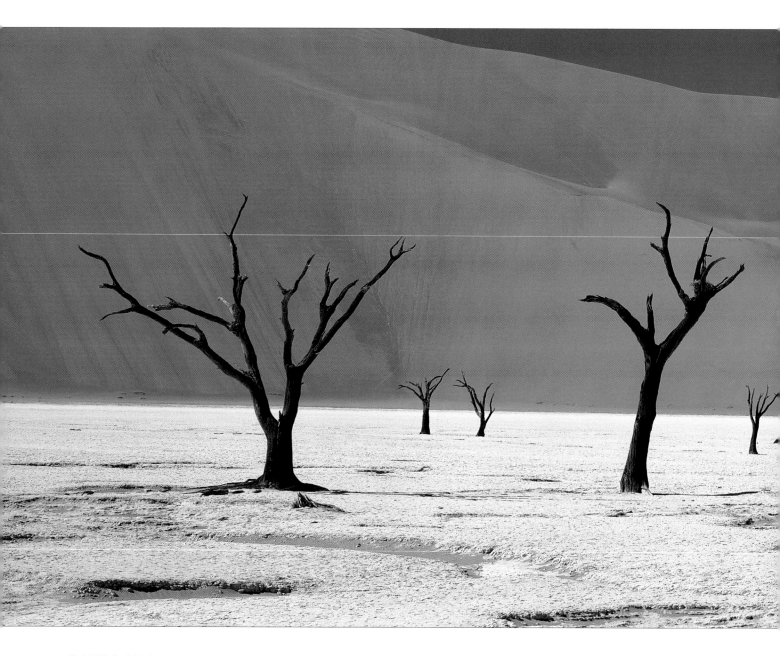

BANDS OF COLOR

This dramatic tableau has no shadows to add a sense of depth, and the photograph has a stark, contemporary feel. The order and balance dictated by the first six trees on the left compensates for the untidy right-hand-side of the photograph.

Location: NAMIBIA, AFRICA

Camera: 6cm x 17cm; Lens: 300mm; Film: Fuji 50 ASA; Exposure: 2 seconds at f.64

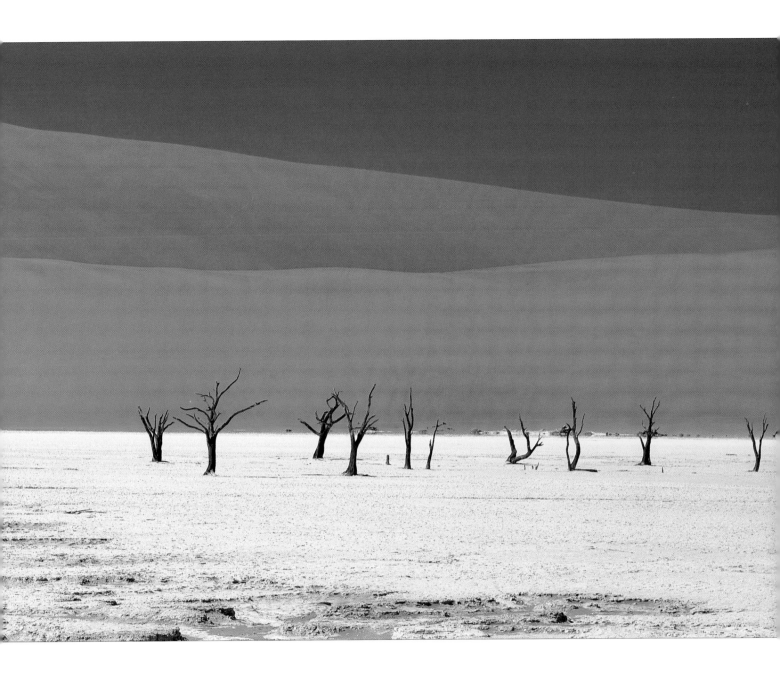

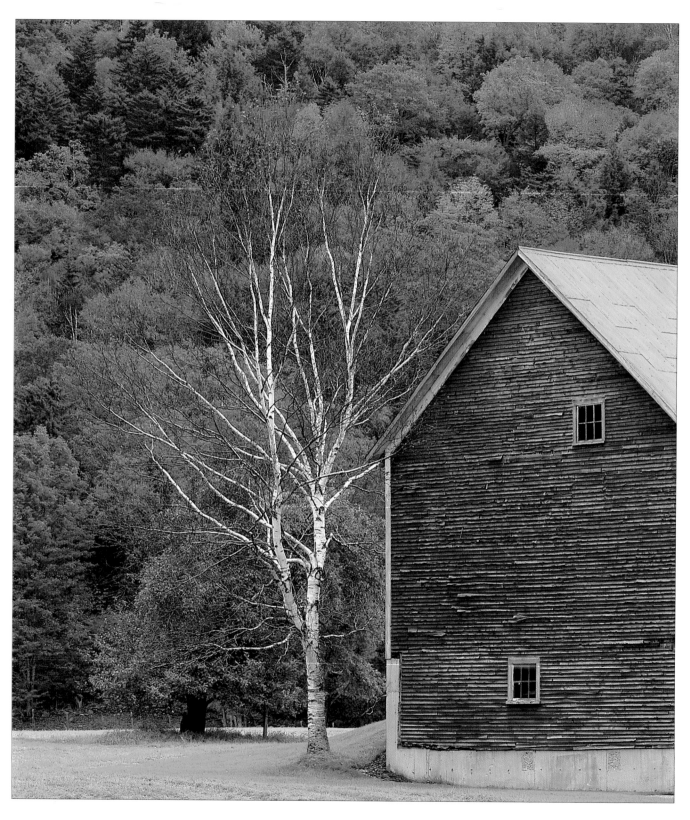

A GHOSTLY TREE

Here the frame edge slices through the barn, but I like the shapes and angles. I was drawn by the peeling paint, the windows, and the milky roof. The red paint contains a whiteness that echoes the silvery silhouette of the tree. Remember what it was that first drew you to an image, and retain a sense of that in the final photograph.

Location: VERMONT, USA

Camera: 6cm x 6cm;
Lens: 150mm;
Film: Fuji 50 ASA;
Exposure: ½ second at f.32;
Filter: 81A (warm up)

IMPRESSIONIST POPPIES

I fell in love with this house. I used a fast film to produce a soft, grainy effect. It falls into bands of color pivoted around a central horizon. Everything is impressionistically rendered, the stalks and bearded heads of the barley, giving the foreground a brushy feel.

Location: TUSCANY, ITALY

Camera: 35mm;
Lens: 150mm;
Film: Agfa 1000 ASA;
Exposure: ¹⁄₆₀ second at f.22

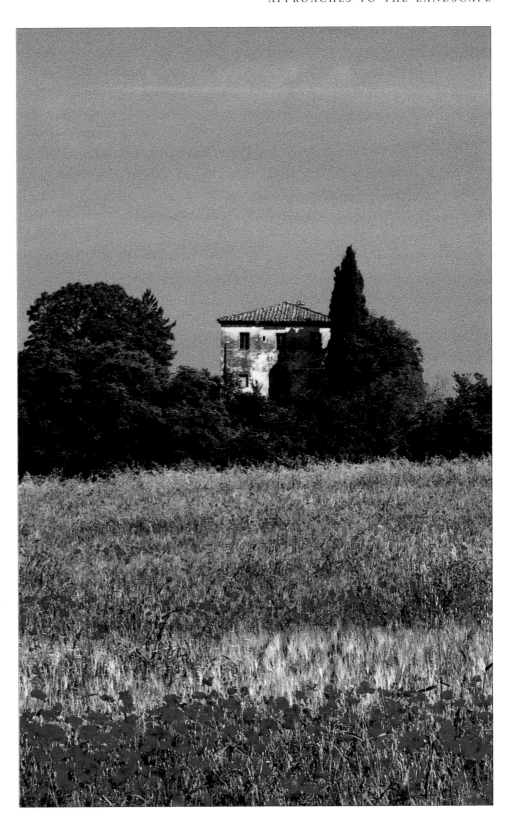

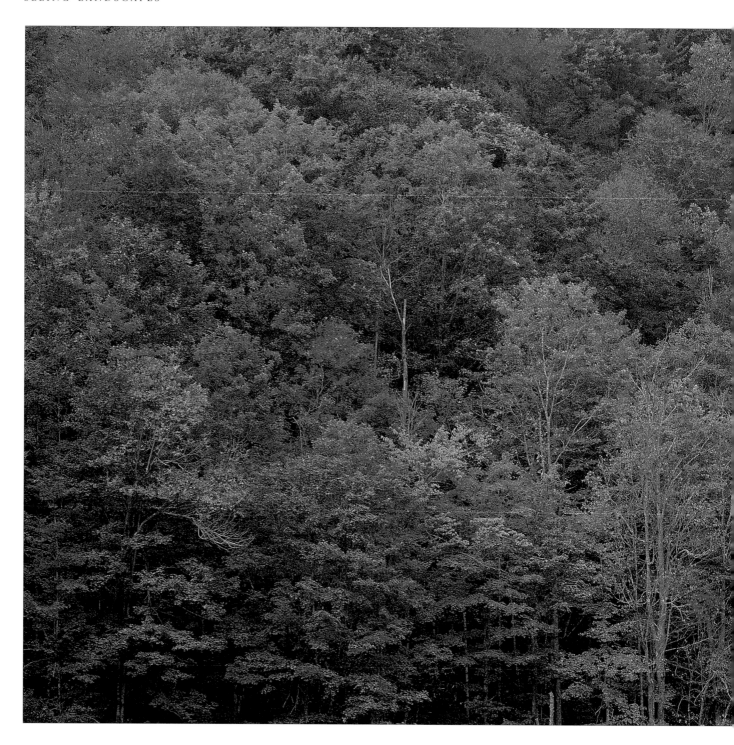

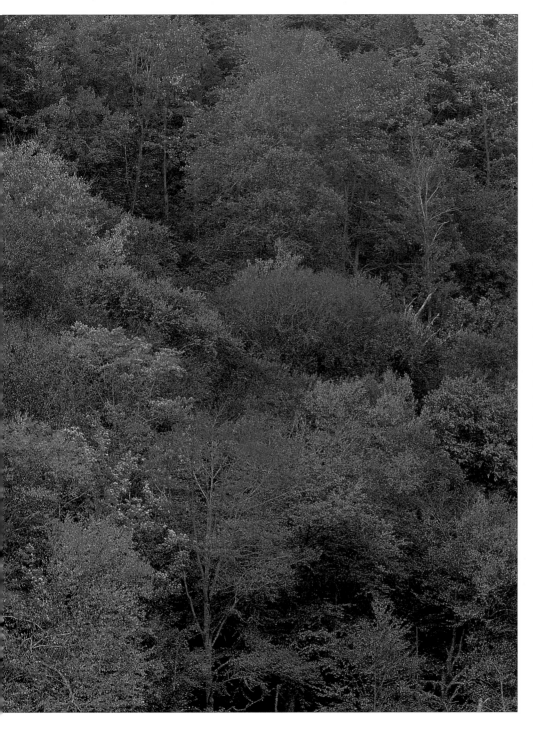

COMPRESSED COLORS

In this image I deliberately played up the decorative qualities of fall colors. By coming in tight to trees ranged up a hillside I have created a shallow picture space in which there is little recession and few clues to the spatial relationships. The trunks of the trees are not visible and the crowns of the trees overlap and repeat across the image to create a gorgeous tapestry of color and texture.

Location: VERMONT, USA

Camera: 6cm x 17cm,
cropped image;
Lens: 300mm;
Film: Fuji 50 ASA;
Exposure: ½ second at f.32

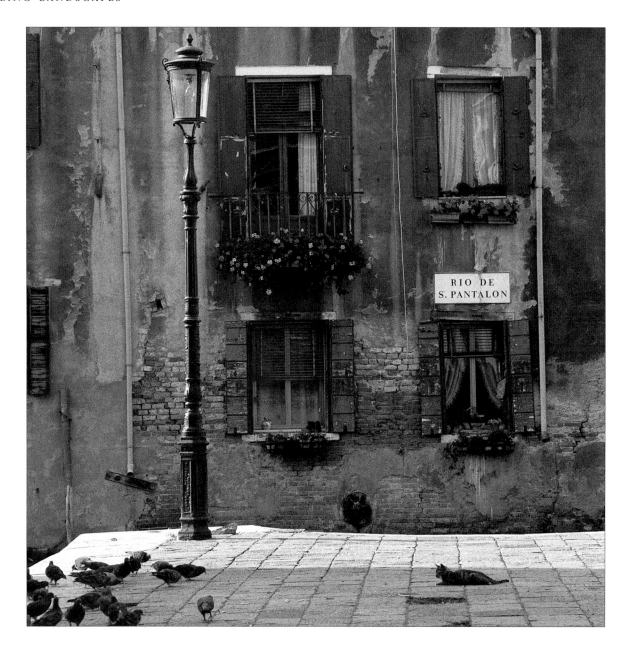

PAINTERLY EFFECT

The decaying charm of Venice responds well to a coarse-grained film. The paving stones recede from the viewer and provide a stage for the silent drama being played out between the cat and the pigeons. By a happy chance the light sneaking in between the buildings makes the gaslight look as though it is lit.

Location: VENICE, ITALY

Camera: 6cm x 6cm; Lens: 50mm; Film: Agfa 1000 ASA; Exposure: 1/60 second at f.22

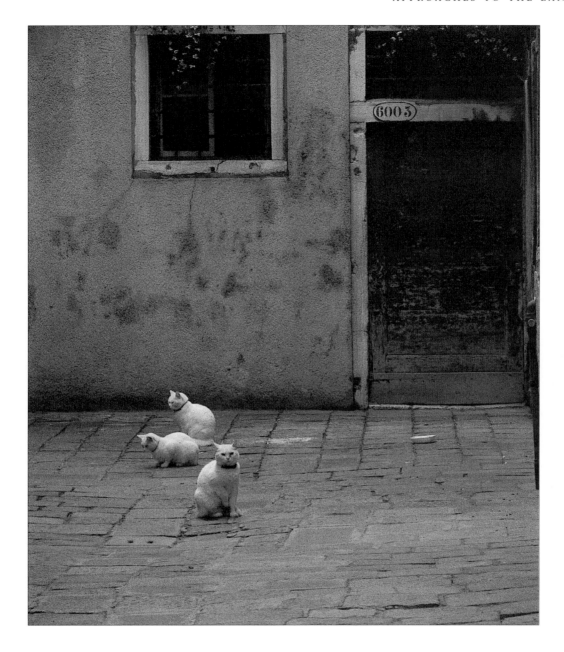

TIMELESS MOOD

I've used a 1000 ASA film again to create a still mood and emphasize the textures and muted colors. At fast speeds film is less predictable, and here it has distorted the colors so the cats have a mauve tinge.

Location: VENICE, ITALY

Camera: 6cm x 6cm; Lens: 50mm; Film: Agfa 1000 ASA;
Exposure: $\frac{1}{125}$ second at f.22

PRIMARY COLORS

A meadow of flowers is spiritually uplifting, but getting that across on film is a challenge, as the camera is more critical than the eye. I spent a lot of time finding a section where the flowers and colors were evenly distributed so that I could capture the profusion and color of the original.

Location: ANDALUSIA, SPAIN

Camera: 6cm x 6cm; Lens: 150mm; Film: Fuji 100 ASA; Exposure: ⅛ second at f.32; Filter: polarizer

SELECTIVE DISTRIBUTION

I was thrilled when I found this field of flowers. Again I had to get up my ladder to find an all-over pattern that was evenly distributed. I experimented with a slightly soft focus so that the photograph would express the total effect rather than the individuality of each flower.

Location: ANDALUSIA, SPAIN

Camera: 6cm x 6cm; Lens: 250mm; Film: Fuji 50 ASA; Exposure: ¼ second at f.45; Filters: polarizer, soft

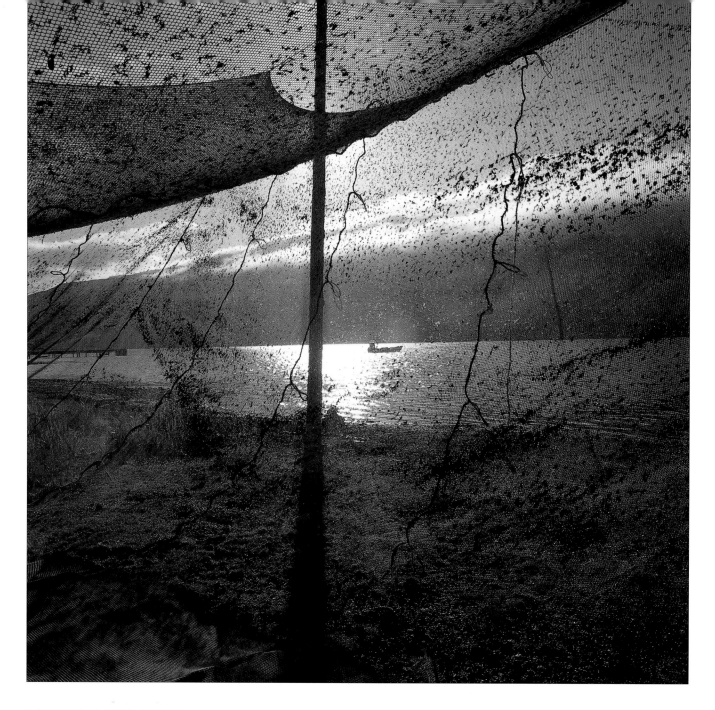

DIFFUSING THE SCENE

I felt that I must do something with this marvellous net, the gorgeous light, and the weird, banked-up clouds. The diffuse image looks almost impressionistic. It took me 45 minutes to 'find' my picture. The wooden stake is an important feature of the composition, its emphatic uprightness is a nice contrast to the other elements that are primarily soft and have a lateral stress – I also used it to prevent the sun from shining into the lens.

Location: HIGHLANDS, SCOTLAND

Camera: 6cm x 6cm; Lens: 50mm; Film: Fuji 50 ASA; Exposure: ⅓₀ second at f.8

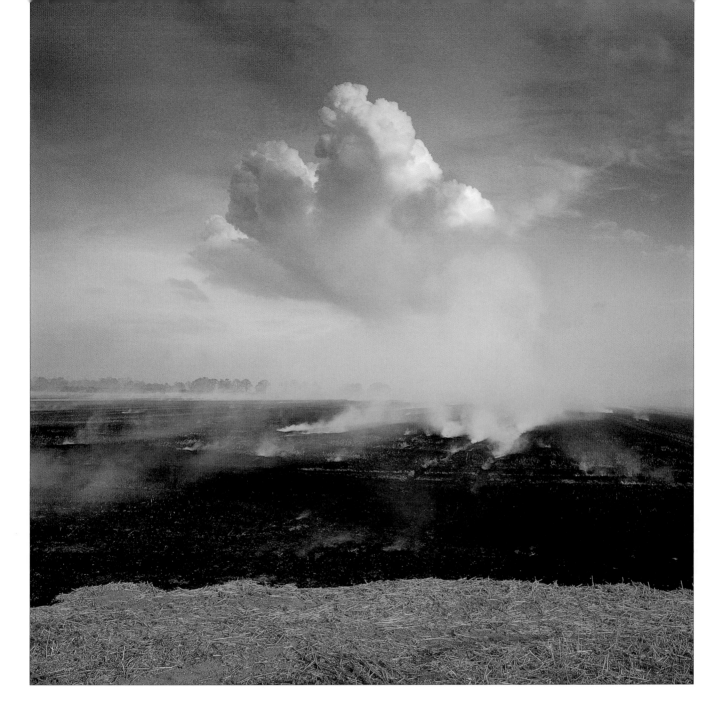

SMOKE SCREEN

This strange picture took no more than five minutes to capture. The cloud of smoke and vapor was hanging over the burning stubble. The peaty browns of the scorched earth and the wisps of smoke had a disturbing feel. The cloud dissolved after four or five minutes. The farmer was standing mesmerized by the scene – he too had never seen anything like it.

Location: LINCOLNSHIRE, ENGLAND

Camera: 6cm x 6cm; Lens: 50mm; Film: Kodak 64 ASA; Exposure: ⅟₃₀ second at f.8–11

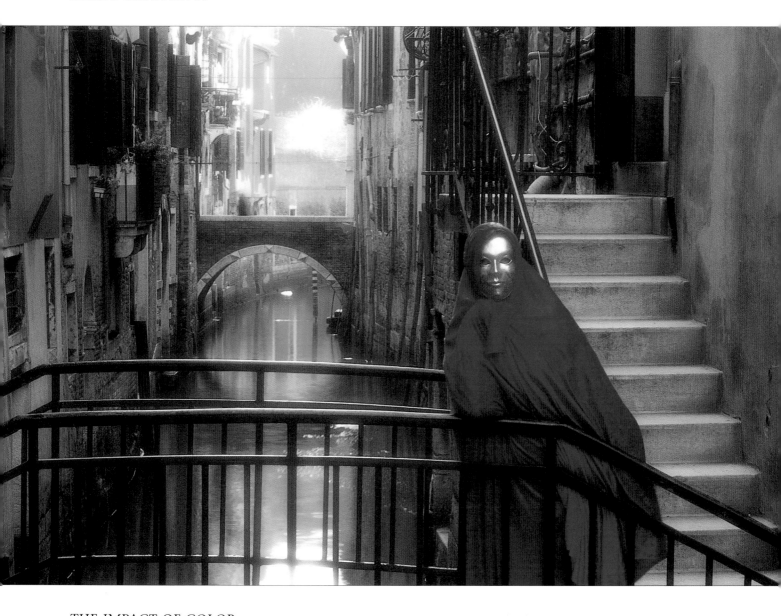

THE IMPACT OF COLOR

The masked figures of carnival are disconcerting and strange, and look marvellous set against the theatrical decay of the city of Venice. In this version the eye travels along the canal to the lovely golden light falling on the pink- and butter-colored plaster. The pervading cool shadows provide a neutral foil for the gorgeous crimson figure.

Location: VENICE, ITALY

Camera: 35mm; Lens: 105mm; Film: Fuji 50 ASA; Exposure: ¼ second at f.22

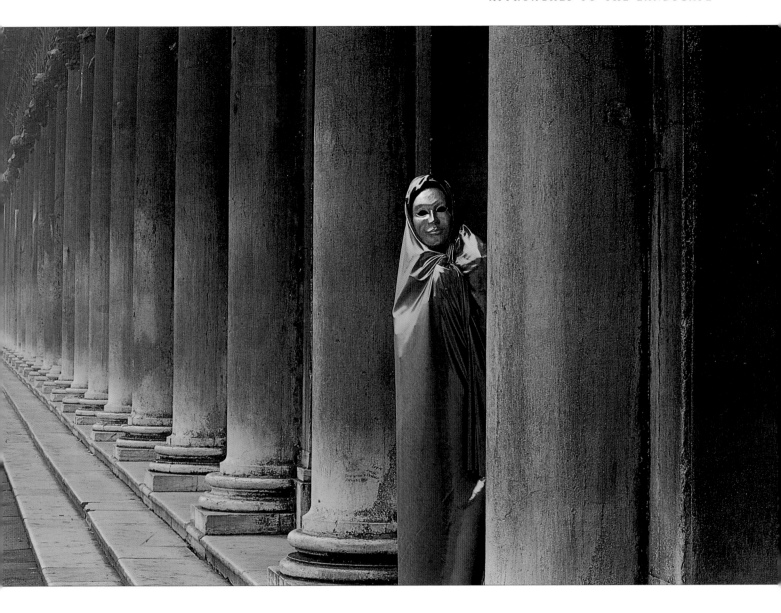

DISRUPTING THE MONOCHROME

The austere repetitions of the classical columns that border St Mark's Square create
an entirely different mood. I chose a viewpoint that excluded any spaces, so that the
columns rippled into the distance. The dull gold of the carnival figure provides a
contrast and injects a sense of drama, which is entirely appropriate in this scene.

Location: VENICE, ITALY

Camera: 35mm; Lens: 135mm; Film: Fuji 50 ASA; Exposure: 1 second at f.22

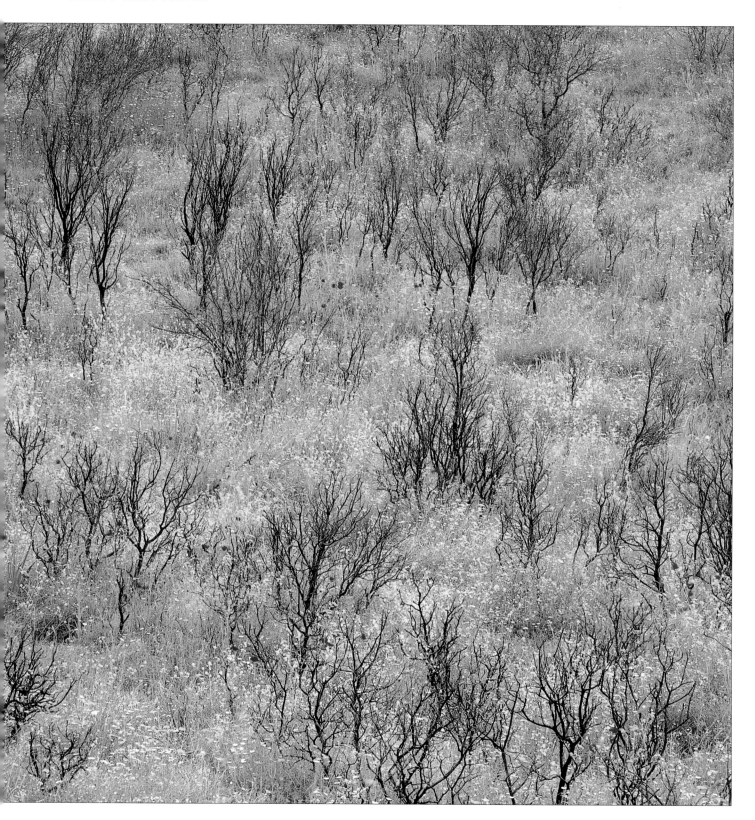

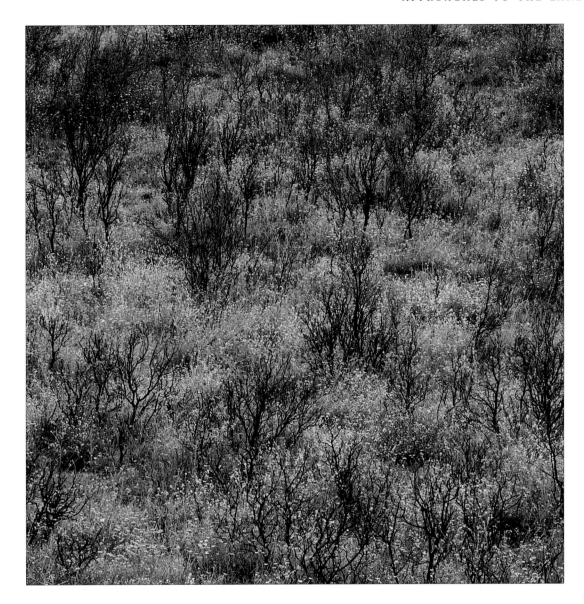

SCORCHED SAPLINGS: SLOW FILM

These saplings were burnt in a fire, but the earth recovered and produced this profusion of flowers. The flowers and foliage are a wonderful contrast to the black, skeletal trees. I wanted to find a repeating pattern, so I explored different viewpoints and used a ladder to give me height.

Location: CIUDAD REAL, SPAIN

Camera: 6cm x 6cm; Lens: 150mm;
Film: Fuji 50 ASA; Exposure: ¼ second at f.22

SCORCHED SAPLINGS: FAST FILM

This is the same image taken three minutes later with 1000 ASA film. This comparison illustrates the effect of a fast film. The colors are more muted and less contrasted than in the version shot with 50 ASA fine-grained film. The grainy texture gives the image a less precise feel.

Location: CIUDAD REAL, SPAIN

Camera: 6cm x 6cm; Lens: 150mm;
Film: Agfa 1000 ASA; Exposure: ⅟₆₀ second at f.22

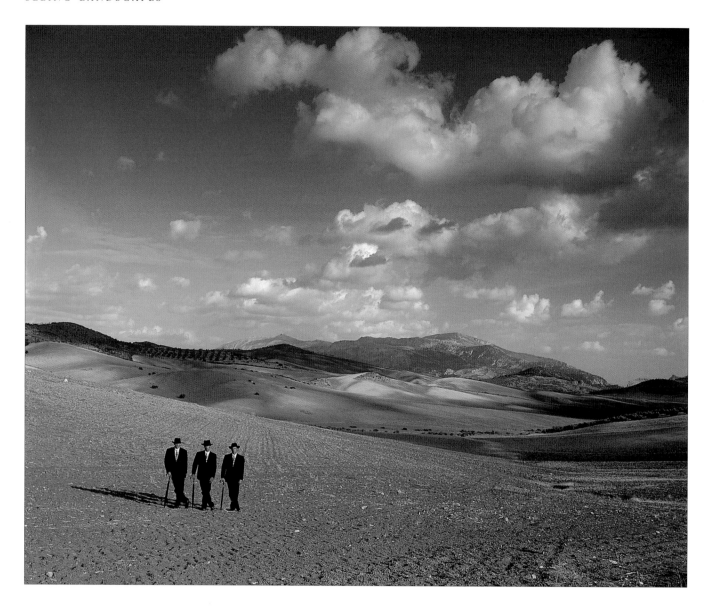

INTRODUCING THE UNEXPECTED: 1

This pair of photographs was a commission and the two images have a deliberately surreal quality. Three smart figures have been planted in a barren landscape. They are looking directly to the camera and the late-afternoon light casts crisp dark shadows. The intention is to disconcert the viewer to ask why and how they came to be in that place. The figures could have been smaller and the image would still have worked in the same way.

Location: ANDALUSIA, SPAIN

Camera: 6cm x 6cm; Lens: 50mm; Film: Fuji 100 ASA;
Exposure: ⅓₀ second at f.11–16; Filters: polarizer, low-density, graduated

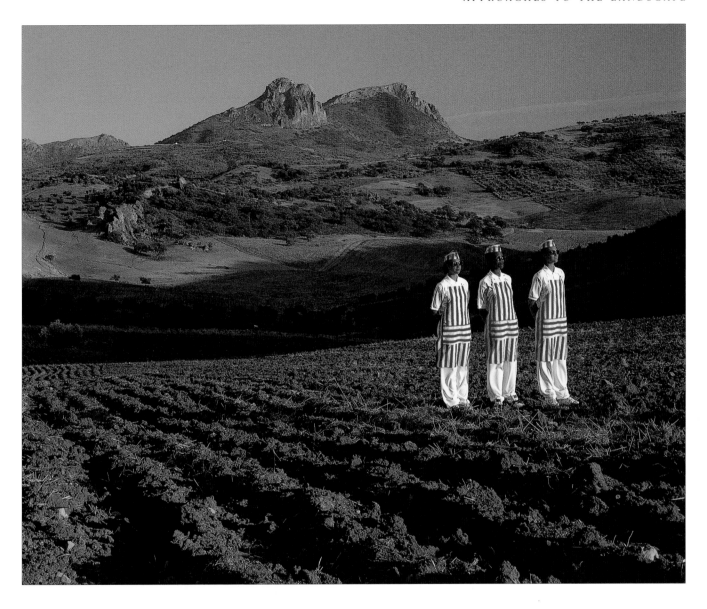

INTRODUCING THE UNEXPECTED: 2

Putting people dressed as fast-food staff into a big landscape seemed as bizarre as you could get. Their red and white uniforms stand out against the neutral earth tones of the background. Their sunglasses were a deliberate device designed to give them a strange, alien appearance and I spent a while ensuring that the sun glinted on their sunglasses.

Location: ANDALUSIA, SPAIN

Camera: 6cm x 6cm; Lens: 50mm; Film: Fuji 50 ASA;
Exposure: ¹⁄₁₅ second at f.11; Filter: polarizer

141

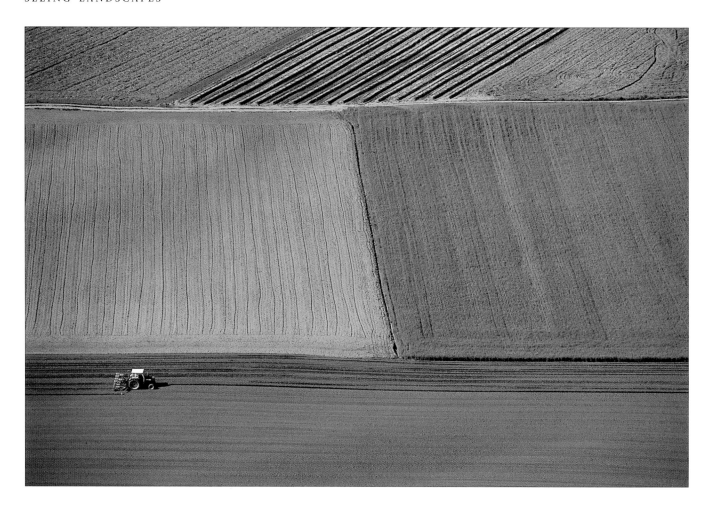

PARTIAL ABSTRACTION

I took this pair of photographs from a hilltop village –
I was about 800ft (240m) up, so they are almost aerial
views. I've been very selective, as these regular blocks of
color were hidden amongst a lot of unruly shapes. In this
version the tractor gives a sense of scale and provides a
clue as to what we are looking at, putting the photograph
into context. The farmer took about 20 minutes to get
from one of the fields to the other, so there were long
waits between shots.

Location: DORDOGNE, FRANCE

Camera: 35mm; Lens: 200mm; Film: Fuji 100 ASA;
Exposure: ¹⁄₃₀ second at f.11; Filter: polarizer

COMPLETE ABSTRACTION

A high viewpoint flattens and abstracts the landscape, so
we see a jigsaw of interlocking forms. Without sky, or any
clues to recession, there is no sense of space. In the picture
opposite, the tractor provides a clue to scale and subject –
here the landscape becomes an abstraction. The striations
of cultivation add interesting textures.

Location: DORDOGNE, FRANCE

Camera: 35mm; Lens: 200mm; Film: Fuji 100 ASA;
Exposure: 1/30 second at f.11; Filter: polarizer

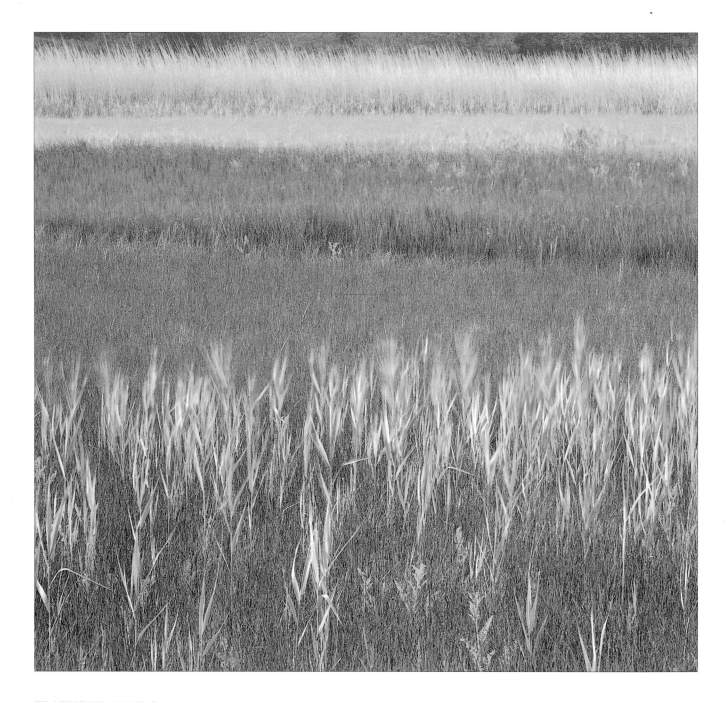

FEATHERY BANDS

I found this pattern of colors and textures on a rainy day. I was looking across a broad vista to the foothills and mountains beyond, when I saw this picture. I contracted my vision to a small area, and removed a segment of landscape from its context.

Location: LUGO, SPAIN

Camera: 6cm x 6cm; Lens: 150mm; Film: Fuji 50 ASA; Exposure: ¼ second at f.32

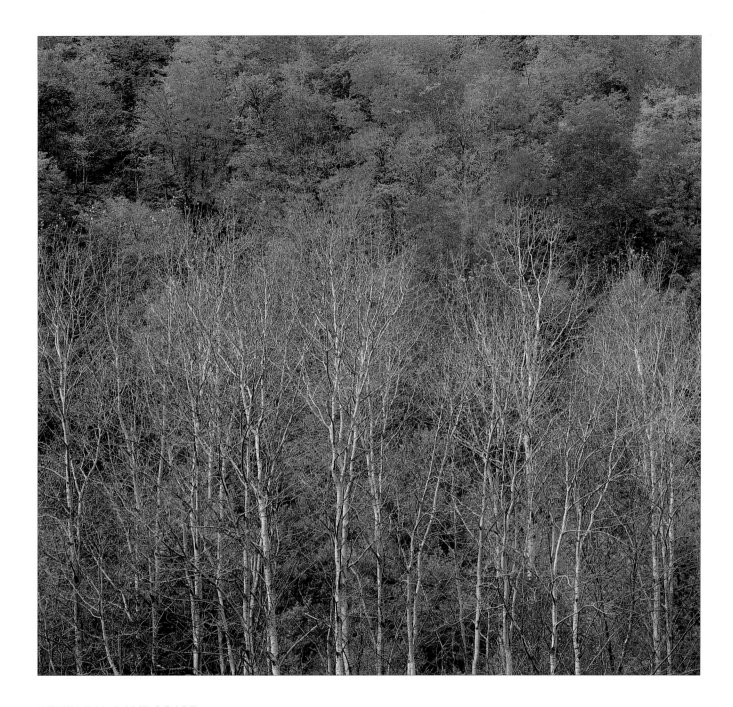

ETHEREAL LANDSCAPE

This row of silver birches was set against a very steep bank. They are almost entirely devoid of leaves, yet the trees beyond are fully clothed. The delicate tracery of the birches contrasts with the rich colors of those behind.

Location: VERMONT, USA

Camera: 6cm x 6cm; Lens: 150mm; Film: Fuji 100 ASA;
Exposure: ⅟₁₅ second at f.16; Filter: 81B (warm up)

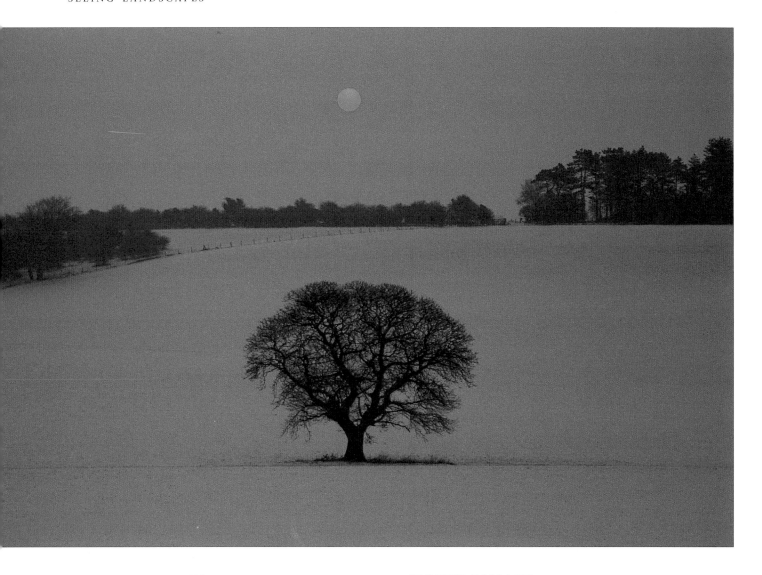

THROUGH THE MIST

The morning sun coming through fog creates a strangely eerie landscape. The sun, a luminous orange orb, looks unreal, like a lantern suspended in the sky. The oak tree falls directly beneath the sun and is crisply outlined by the snowy-blanketed field. The early light gives the scene a cool mauve cast, which heightens the orange of the sun.

Location: WILTSHIRE, ENGLAND

Camera: 35mm; Lens: 300mm; Film: Fuji 100 ASA;
Exposure: ¹⁄₁₅ second at f.16

SPOTLIT FOLIAGE

Isolated on its hilltop, a single tree is turned to glorious gold by a shaft of directional light. The topmost branches, which are bending in the wind, emphasize the exposed nature of the location, while the sparkling light suggests the transient effects of weather. I have cropped in tight to eliminate a path that would undermine the sense of remoteness I was seeking to convey.

Location: HIGHLANDS, SCOTLAND

Camera: 6cm x 6cm; Lens: 250mm; Film: Fuji 100 ASA;
Exposure: ¹⁄₁₅ second at f.16–22; Filter: polarizer

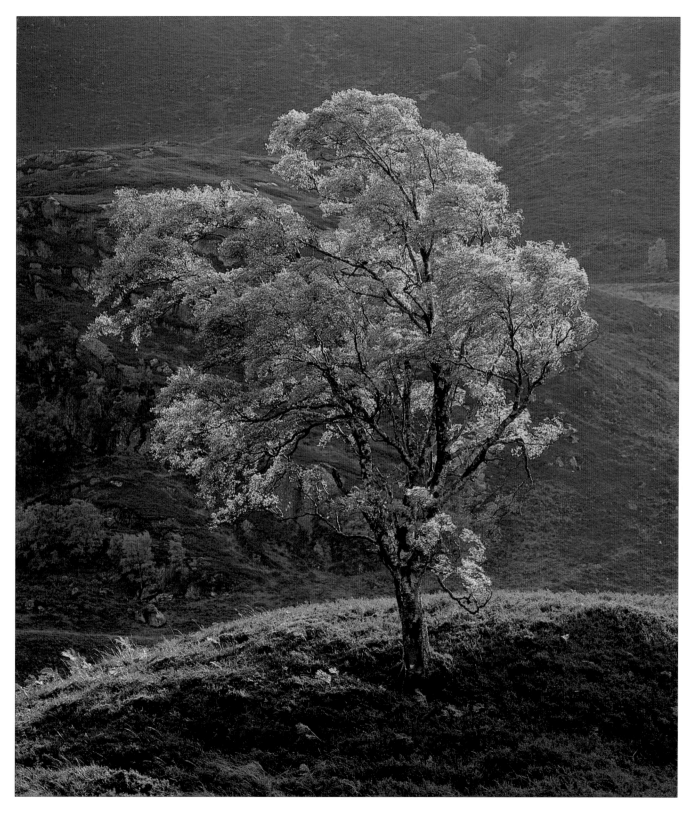

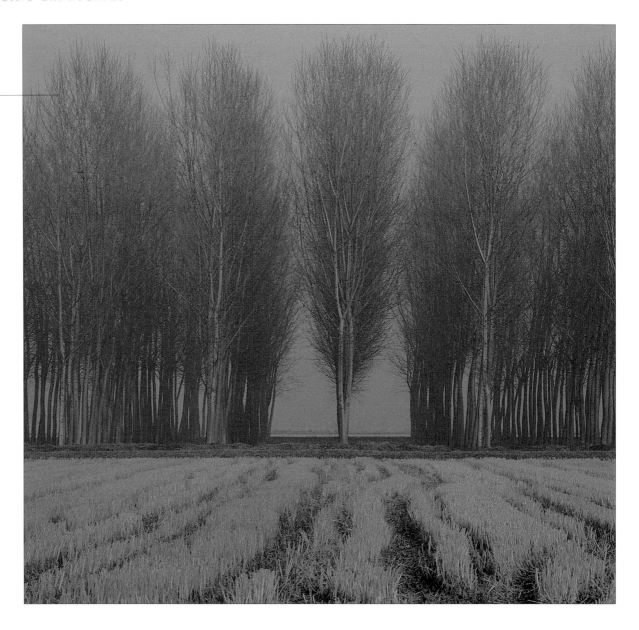

MINIMAL LIGHT

This is the flattest light I have ever worked in and shows that photography can
work with only a little light. It was freezing cold and the fog was beginning to roll
in. I was attracted by the symmetry and height of these trees seen through a fine
mist and the way the tracks in the stubble led to the poplars. The mist and the
evening light envelop the image in a hazy veil, which produces visual harmony.

Location: Provence, France

Camera: 6cm x 6cm; Lens: 150mm; Film: Fuji 50 ASA; Exposure: 1 second at f.32

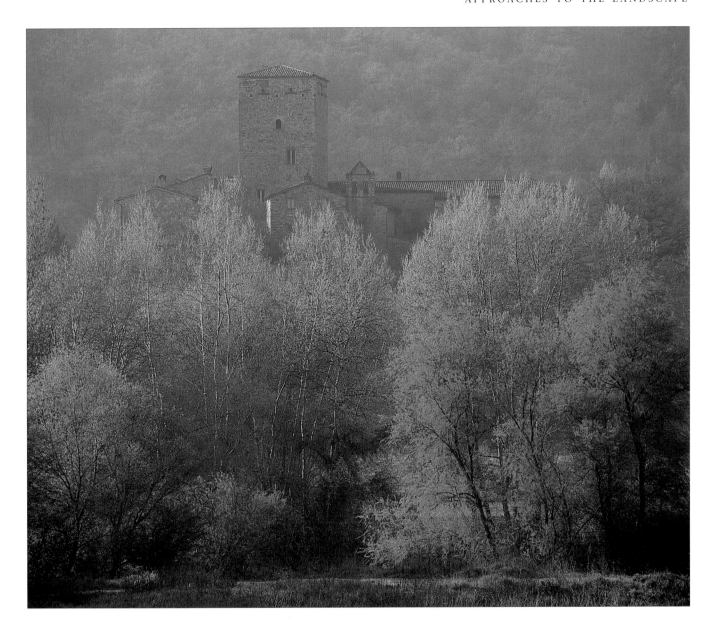

MORNING LIGHT

The soft morning light subdues color and tone, creating a sense of harmony where there is actually very little order. The light skims the delicate foliage of the trees and sparkles on their bark. The different elements of the image are not clearly defined – even the village is camouflaged and blends into the overall vista. A splash of light glimmers below the tower.

Location: UMBRIA, ITALY

Camera: 6cm x 6cm; Lens: 150mm; Film: Fuji 50 ASA;
Exposure: ½ second at f.22; Filter: 81B (warm up)

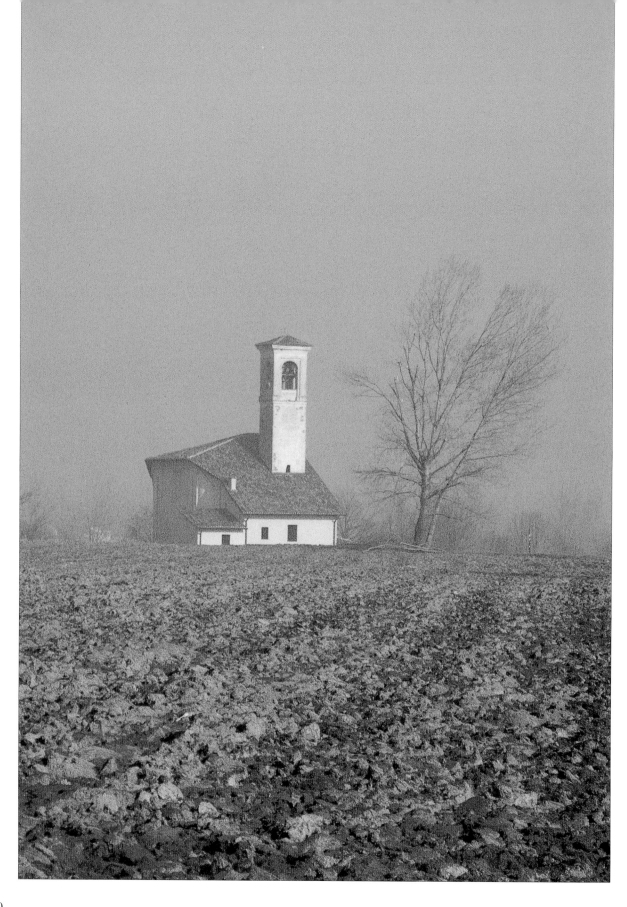

WINTER LIGHT

It was a cold winter day, the colors were muted and the light was not ideal. A fast film emphasized the flat morning light and the bleached colors. A fine-grained film would not have suited the mood. A long lens compressed the field of vision and brought the clods of earth closer to the viewer – they also match the roof's texture.

Location: LOMBARDY, ITALY

Camera: 6cm x 6cm;
Lens: 150mm;
Film: Agfa 1000 ASA;
Exposure: ⅟₆₀ second at f.22–32

PLEASING SHAPE

This is a celebration of a beautiful fence. It snakes over the hill and disappears, and for some reason it fills me with hope. There is a limited color palette, and the soft grass is a contrast to the precise fence. The graininess of a fast film was right for the textures and tones – and gives the image a painterly feel.

Location: BORDERS, SCOTLAND

Camera: 6cm x 6cm;
Lens: 150mm;
Film: Agfa 1000 ASA;
Exposure: ⅟₁₂₅ second at f.32

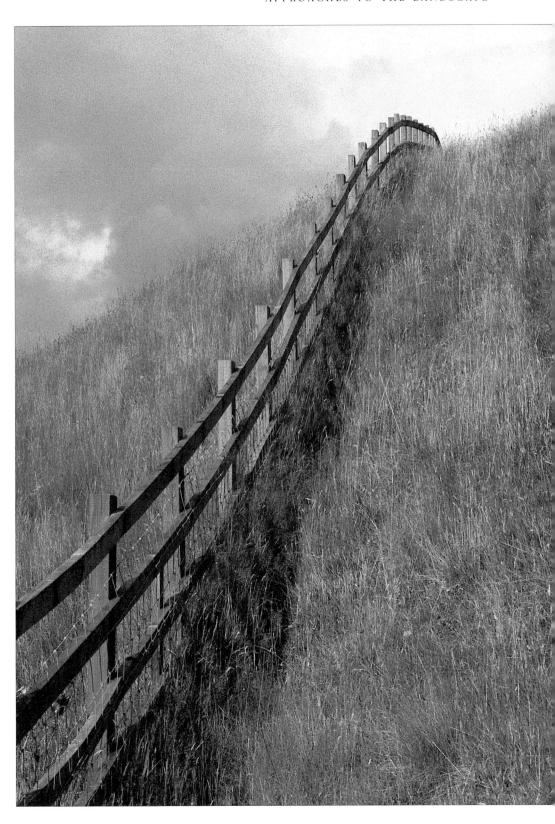

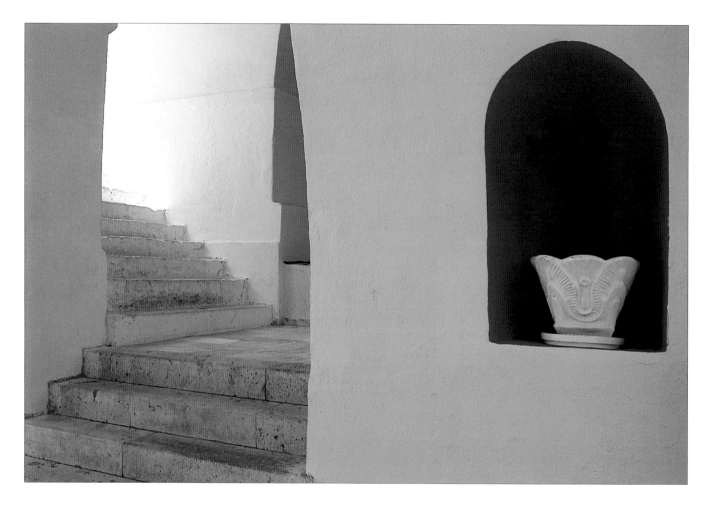

GRAPHIC ELEMENTS

A flight of steps always creates a seductive image. They have a simple, satisfying geometry, create a feeling of movement, and suggest spaces beyond our view. This subject also works as a study of the way white responds to different light conditions. The marvellous blue of the niche provides a striking contrast, and I like the touch of daylight coming through at the top of the stairs.

Location: SÁMOS, GREECE

Camera: 35mm; Lens: 35mm; Film: Fuji 50 ASA; Exposure: ⅟₁₅ second at f.11

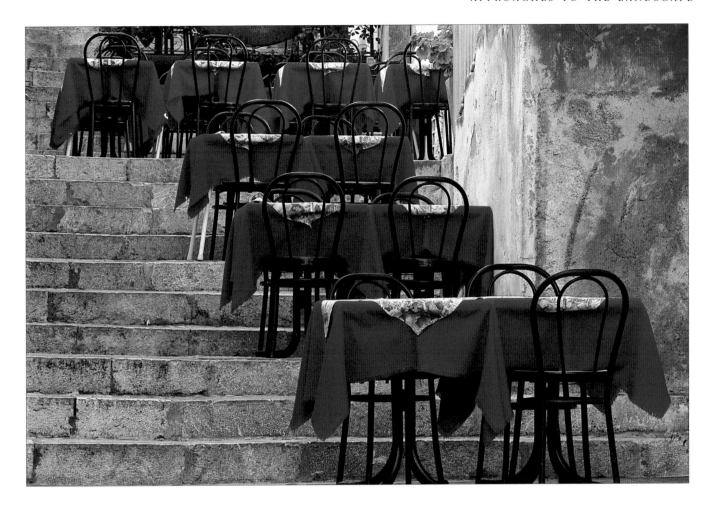

DRAMATIC CASCADE

This cascade of crimson-covered tables makes a striking image. The strong diagonal, the repetition of steps, chairs, tables, and tablecloths has a formal quality. The red cloths sizzle against the predominant neutrals of stucco and stone. It took me 45 minutes to get this picture because as soon as I decided to take a photograph so did everyone else. Unfortunately they wanted their friends to pose on the steps or at the table.

Location: SICILY, ITALY

Camera: 35mm; Lens: 150mm; Film: Fuji 50 ASA;
Exposure: 1/30 second at f.11; Filter: polarizer

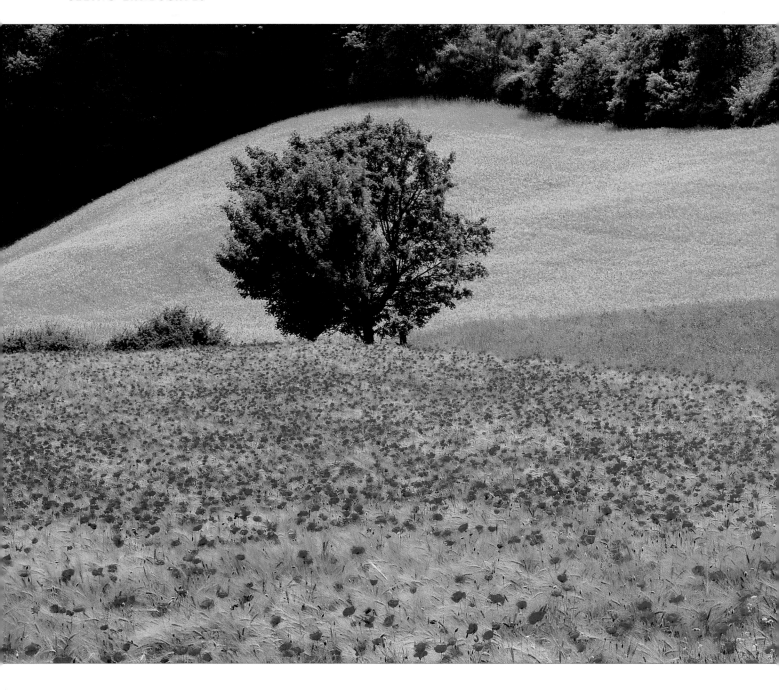

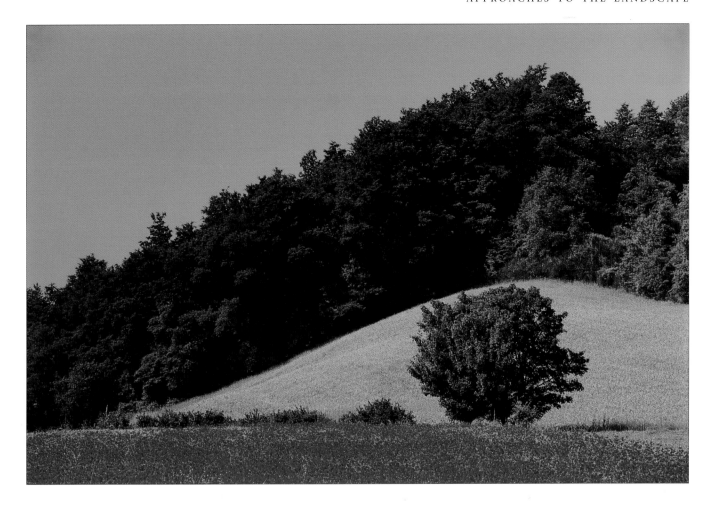

HARMONIOUS SHAPES: 1

In this image I like the shape of the hill, the way the trees hug its contour, the texture and colors of poppies and not-ripe barley, and the way the compact little tree falls so neatly within the slope beyond. In this version I used a long lens to go in close. It brings out the delicate beards of the barley and permits me to crop out the sky. This version has an intimate, contained quality.

Location: TUSCANY, ITALY

Camera: 6cm x 6cm; Lens: 250mm; Film: Fuji 50 ASA; Exposure: ⅛ second at f.32

HARMONIOUS SHAPES: 2

Although this version includes more landscape and sky, it has a pared down, graphic quality. It was taken a week earlier than the one on the facing page. The foreground becomes a solid mass of red, while the woods form a solid swathe over the hill. I needed a ladder to prevent the little tree from invading the wooded area at the top.

Location: TUSCANY, ITALY

Camera: 35mm; Lens: 180mm; Film: Fuji 50 ASA; Exposure: ⅟₃₀ second at f.22–32

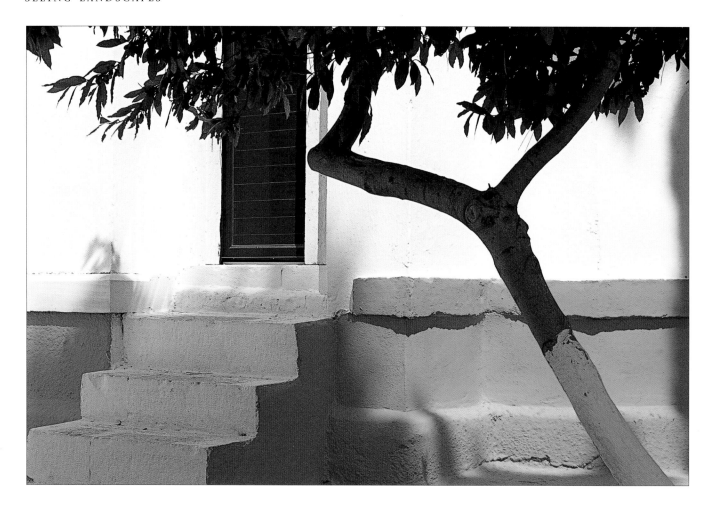

MYSTERIOUS SHADOWS: 1

This monastery in Greece provided a visual banquet and I took many photographs. Everything was appealing – the architecture, the colors, the light. In this little scene the colors are arranged as blocks so it has an abstract quality. The silhouette of the tree makes wonderfully graphic shapes, although I had to work hard to prevent the elbow of the branch from invading the door. The shadows give a powerful sense of the sunlight beyond.

Location: SÁMOS, GREECE

Camera: 35mm; Lens: 28mm; Film: Fuji 50 ASA; Exposure: $\frac{1}{30}$ second at f.11; Filter: polarizer

MYSTERIOUS SHADOWS: 2

Strong light on architecture tends to emphasize the formal qualities that underpin the structure. Here, the light and dark on the steps make a diagonal of stripes. The eye is drawn to the bordering wall, which receives the full force of the light and contrasts with the darkness behind. I like the shadow of the figure seated on the steps with the newspaper because it suggests a presence that is beyond the picture space.

Location: VENICE, ITALY

Camera: 6cm x 6cm; Lens: 50mm; Film: Fuji 100 ASA; Exposure: $\frac{1}{15}$ second at f.16

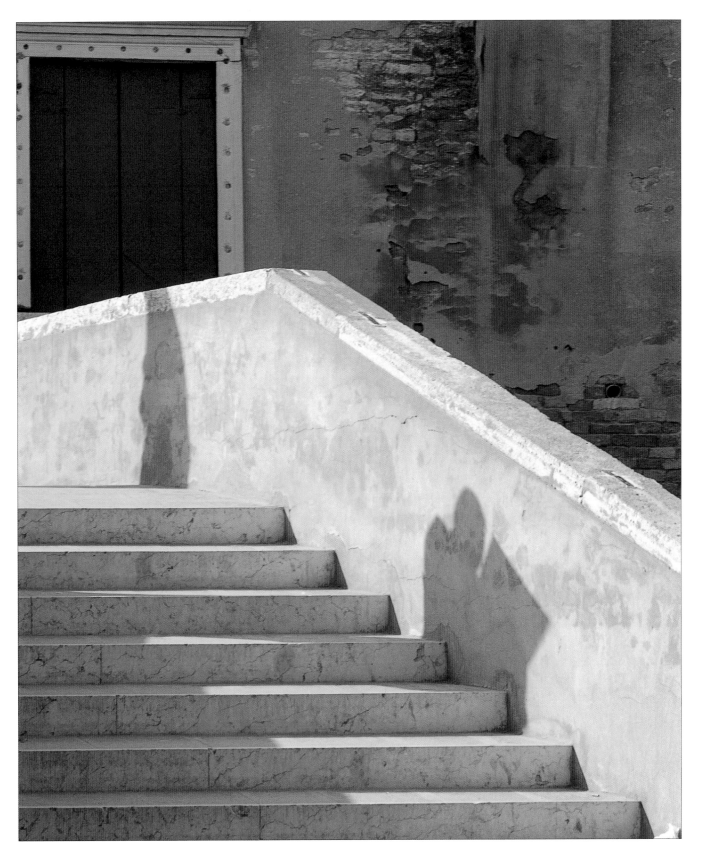

Index

Acknowledgements

Much gratitude is due to Patricia Monahan for all her patience, enthusiasm and friendship. Thanks also to Sarah Hoggett, Claire Graham and Corinne Asghar at Collins & Brown for their guidance and encouragement.